A Radical Proposal

Christ-Centered Ministry

versus

Problem-Centered Counseling

Martin and Deidre Bobgan

Scripture quotations are taken from the
Authorized King James Version of the Bible.

**Christ-Centered Ministry versus
Problem-Centered Counseling**

Copyright © 2004 Martin and Deidre Bobgan
Published by EastGate Publishers
4137 Primavera Road
Santa Barbara, California 93110

Library of Congress Catalog Card Number 2003098701
ISBN 0-941717-19-4

Printed in the United States of America

Then said they unto him, What shall we do, that we might work the works of God? Jesus answered and said unto them, This is the work of God, that ye believe on him whom he hath sent (John 6:28,29).

Abide in me, and I in you. As the branch cannot bear fruit of itself, except it abide in the vine; no more can ye, except ye abide in me. I am the vine, ye are the branches: He that abideth in me, and I in him, the same bringeth forth much fruit: for without me ye can do nothing (John 15:4,5).

For a sample copy of a free newsletter about the intrusion of psychological counseling theories and therapies into the church, please write to:

PsychoHeresy Awareness Ministries
4137 Primavera Road
Santa Barbara, CA 93110

or call:

1-800-216-4696

<http://www.psychoheresy-aware.org>

Table of Contents

1

A Radical Proposal

Many years ago we traveled through the dark terrain of psychology hoping to discover the secrets of human nature and how to help people suffering from problems of living. The more we searched through the theories and therapies of counseling psychology, the more we saw its fallacies, failures, and false ways. It was not until the bright light of the Gospel shined in our lives that we saw hope for mankind and the true answer to problems of living! Our confidence in the conversation of counseling to help people solve problems of living shifted from the psychological way to what we thought was the spiritual way. We became part of the biblical counseling movement until we realized that in many ways it simply reflected the psychological way.

In this book we use the terms *counselor, counselee*, and *counseling* when we are speaking about either psychological or biblical counseling since these are the terms they use. However, when we refer to those individuals engaged in Christ-centered ministry, we will identify the one who ministers with terms such as the *helper* or *servant* rather than *counselor*, the one who is seeking help as the *seeker* or *fellow believer* rather than *counselee*, and *ministry*, *ministering*, or *mutual care* rather than *counseling*.

Counseling involves two or more people conversing about problems with one being the so-called expert (counselor) who is expected to provide answers and solutions for the one in need (counselee). The desire to help people who are suffering from problems of living quickly translates into focusing on the person and the problem. Thus much of both psychological and biblical counseling focuses attention on people and their problems. The goal easily becomes solving the problem rather than spiritual growth and the center of attention becomes the person and the problem more than "Christ in you the hope of glory" (Col. 1:27). Throughout Scripture problems of living are shown to be opportunities for spiritual growth. **Problems of living are like torn up ground in a person's life during which the Lord can work mightily through His Word, the Holy Spirit, and the Body of Christ.** Will they be used as such? And how can fellow believers encourage such spiritual growth? How might we all edify one another and encourage one another to trust the Holy Spirit to empower all believers to walk according to their new life in Christ?

In addition to discarding theories and therapies of psychological counseling, **we are discouraging all problem-centered counseling**, whether psychological or biblical. Although this may seem to be a radical move, we contend that as long as personal ministry remains problem-centered and therefore person-focused there will be less spiritual growth and more superficial fixing of the flesh. When such counseling attempts to change behavior, it can end up being a type of behaviorism that cleans the "cup" on the outside (Matt. 23:25) and thereby strengthens the flesh. When such counseling attempts to go deeper than the problems at hand, humans often usurp the role of the Holy Spirit when they try to gain insight into another person or when they attempt to identify the "idols of the heart."

A Radical Proposal

The radical proposal is to discourage problem-centered counseling and to encourage Christ-centered ministry, to overthrow intimidation from the psychological and biblical counseling movements, and thereby to free believers in local congregations to minister to fellow believers without psychological or biblical counseling manuals, workshops, seminars, degrees, or certificates.

Christ-Centered Ministry

Instead of problem-centered counseling, we propose a Christ-centered, biblical ministry that flows forth from the preaching and teaching of the Word. We will refer to this as *Christ-centered ministry* because the emphasis is on Christ and His work in the believer through the Word of God, the Holy Spirit, and the Body of Christ to the glory of the Father. We want to intensify attention given to what already exists in the local church for every believer to be growing in Christ.

The subject of this book is the Lord's provisions for ministering to people with the same problems of living usually dealt with by mental health professionals and biblical counselors through conversation. **This ministry should be accomplished at the local congregational level by believers who have passed from darkness to light through the death and resurrection of Jesus Christ and who are growing in sanctification by denying self and by recognizing that God uses suffering to purify and mature His children.** All Bible-believing churches should have the resources of teaching, preaching, evangelism, fellowship, and prayer to assist individuals who seek help when they are beset with problems of living.

Instead of communicating the message that local congregations don't know and can't do and that they need outside help or need to go elsewhere for ministry, our message is that local congregations do know and can do, if the Word of God is proclaimed with authority and power and there are believers who are maturing in the faith. There is no need to send people out to counseling or to bring counselors into the church, because what is truly needed should already be available regarding preaching the Gospel, teaching the Word, praying, and fellowshipping with the saints. Therefore churches need to address the following questions: Is the Gospel being preached and taught? Are biblical doctrines having to do with salvation, sanctification, and the believers' walk with the Lord being faithfully taught? Are members studying Scripture? Are those believers who are experiencing problems of living spending time with the Lord in His Word and in prayer, are they desiring to grow in Christ, and are they being encouraged in their faith? Are they fellowshipping with like-minded believers? The resources for loving and serving Christ through times of trial are available to every Christian in the Word of God, in the indwelling Holy Spirit, and in the local body of believers.

Very simply, Christ-centered ministry can be summarized in the words *who*, *what*, *why*, *when*, *where*, and *how*. In a nutshell: The "Who" is Jesus Christ. The "What" is the life of Christ and the written Word of God as applied by the Holy Spirit. The "Why" is the Father's mandate to all believers to minister to one another to make increase of the Body and to edify one another in love that all may be conformed to the image of Christ. The "When" and "Where" are whenever and wherever Jesus involves a member of His local church body to minister to another. The "How" is the supernatural work of the Lord through the believer to minister, by grace through faith, such expressions of love as care, comfort, compassion, mercy, encouragement, exhortation, admonition, instruction in truth, and hospitality. **The *who, what, why, when, where,* and *how* already exist in the Body of Christ, particularly in those churches that faithfully minister the Word and where believers are growing in their**

walk with the Lord. We do not believe in cook-book counseling, but rather in life-lived ministry. We are being generally descriptive, not specifically prescriptive.

Spiritual Growth

Christ-centered ministry relies on the work of the Holy Spirit in a believer's life and therefore emphasizes spiritual growth, whereby the believer walks with the Lord according to the Spirit rather than according to the flesh. Thus, believers are encouraged to live their new life in Christ, which is spiritually alive because the Spirit of Christ lives in them. The source of the new life is God and therefore it is both spiritual and eternal. When believers are walking in the Spirit they are living by grace through faith in the Lord Jesus Christ. They are putting off the old ways of what they were before receiving His life and they are following Jesus in holiness, righteousness, truth, mercy, kindness, goodness, love, joy, peace, longsuffering, patience, humility, temperance, gentleness, faith, forgiveness, and obedience to God. When they are walking in the Spirit, their desire is to know and follow Jesus, and they are growing in their love for God and one another.

Walking in the Spirit also means denying the flesh, which in this context means all the sinful ways that are characteristic of fallen mankind. The flesh is all that a person is before he is born again. The flesh is at war with the Spirit (Gal. 5:16,17). Scripture lists some of the works of the flesh as being "adultery, fornication, uncleanness, lasciviousness, idolatry, witchcraft, hatred, variance, emulations, wrath, strife, seditions, heresies, envyings, murders, drunkenness, revellings" (Gal. 5:19-21), lying, stealing, bitterness, anger, clamour, evil speaking, and malice (Eph. 4: 25-31). In short, the flesh is self wanting its own way at the expense of others and in opposition to God. The flesh is self on the throne instead of God. One can easily see how vital it is for believers to walk in the Spirit and to deny the fleshly self. And yet, when people experience problems of living, they often attempt to deal with them through fleshly means.

Through encouragement to grow in their walk with the Lord and to depend on Him, believers not only learn to deal with current problems; they will also become better prepared for future trials and challenges they have not yet faced. Rather than getting into the habit of looking to another person to fix their lives or solve their problems, believers will become established in their own walk with the Lord and in drawing upon the resources they already have in Christ. All biblical ministry is for the sake of building up believers in Christ so that they can walk pleasing to the Lord, serving Him, thanking Him, and glorifying Him through good times and bad (Phil. 4:12).

Importance of Preaching, Teaching, and Ministering Truth

It is disappointing to see that while churches will take responsibility for preaching the Gospel of salvation, as soon as problems occur, they send individuals elsewhere for help, not realizing that problems provide opportunities for sanctification. In fact, **counseling has all but eclipsed preaching in importance for dealing with life's infirmities**. There is a need to regain greater respect for those local church ministries and teachings that lead to salvation and spiritual growth. Paul declared:

> For the preaching of the cross is to them that perish foolishness; but unto us which are saved it is the power of God (1 Cor. 1:18).

> So, as much as in me is, I am ready to preach the gospel to you that are at Rome also. For I am not ashamed of the gospel of Christ: for it is the power of God unto salvation to every one that believeth; to the Jew first, and also to the Greek. For therein is the righteousness of God revealed from faith to faith: as it is written, The just shall live by faith (Romans 1:15-17).

Preaching and teaching in the local church are God's ministry gifts to bring people to salvation and through sanctification and also to equip the saints for ministering to one another in the Body of Christ (Eph. 4:11,12). **The emphasis is always to be on Christ and what He has done, is doing, and will do in the life of every believer through trials as well as through daily living.** He is the source and resource of both salvation and sanctification. Therefore Paul wrote:

As ye have therefore received Christ Jesus
the Lord, so walk ye in him: Rooted and built
up in him, and stablished in the faith, as ye
have been taught, abounding therein with
thanksgiving. Beware lest any man spoil
you through philosophy and vain deceit,
after the tradition of men, after the rudiments of the world, and not after Christ.
For in him dwelleth all the fulness of the
Godhead bodily (Col. 2:6-9).

We hope to encourage believers to minister to
one another with the attention on Christ, the Word
of God, and the Holy Spirit. The goal of Christ-
centered ministry is spiritual growth in walking
in the Spirit rather than the flesh. We encourage
confidence in the vast provisions of our Lord and
discourage all reliance on counseling systems. We
encourage reliance on the Holy Spirit to enable
believers to minister to one another in the Body
of Christ and reject all forms of intimidation from
the counseling world.

The ideal seeker of Christ-centered ministry
would be one who already knows that problems of
living are opportunities for spiritual growth and
is looking for someone to help utilize what God
has already given in His Word, His indwelling Holy
Spirit, and in the Body of Christ. But these people
are rare, because most Christians have become
culturally accustomed to expect problem-centered
counseling. Not only is our proposal for Christ-
centered ministry instead of problem-centered
counseling radical; even more radical will be imple-
menting these God-given, biblically valid ways of

ministry because of the current fixation on problem-centered counseling.

Preview

Through the years we have documented the faults of psychological counseling and enumerated the errors of the biblical counseling movement in our books and articles.[1] We are not saying that there is no good in either the psychological counseling movement or the biblical counseling movement. Some psychotherapists give good advice and some biblical counselors are truly biblical. We are saying that both movements intimidate believers, focus too much on solving problems, and have enough common and individual faults to reject them.

Many who will read this book have read one or more of our other books and articles and are familiar with our position on psychological and biblical counseling. Nevertheless, we have included some of the reasons we oppose those movements in Chapters Two and Three.

Chapter Two is a brief summary of research evidence that demonstrates how empty the promises of psychotherapy and its underlying psychologies really are. This type of psychology, which purports to help individuals with problems of living, is the very wisdom of men about which God warns His people (1 Cor. 2). While Christians do not need scientific research to convince them that the Lord and His Word give them all they need for life and godliness, it is important to understand that the scientific research does support the Bible but does **not** support the psychological takeover in the church.

Chapter Three reveals weaknesses of the biblical counseling movement and shows parallels between it and its precursor, the psychological counseling movement. Biblical counselors' intent to be as biblical as possible is undermined by their problem-centered counseling, which is a reflection of the psychological counseling movement.

Chapter Four reveals the origins of problem-centered counseling, and Chapter Five explains the differences between Christ-centered ministry and problem-centered counseling. Chapter Six briefly describes the who, what, why, when, where, and how of Christ-centered ministry. Chapter Seven demonstrates advantages of Christ-centered ministry over problem-centered counseling and encourages believers in local congregations to minister to one another according to the Word of God and the indwelling Life of Christ.

Our Purpose

Christ-centered ministry is much broader than counseling. We discuss the broadness of what is included in caring for souls in our book *Competent to Minister*. However, **the purpose of this book is to reveal the origins and faults of problem-centered counseling, to describe Christ-centered ministry and how it differs from problem-centered counseling, and to encourage local congregations to minister as God has called them to do without the influ-**

**ence of the psychological or biblical coun-
seling movements.** Much of what we say will be
familiar to Christians. But, the call for those
mature in the faith to be salt and light in the local
church in the current era of licensed psychological counselors and degreed or certificated biblical
counselors will contrast with what currently exists
in the church world. While this book is aimed at
encouraging believers who are maturing in the
faith to minister to one another in their local
congregations, it also encourages all believers to
grow spiritually in faith and practice.

While we have titled this chapter "A Radical
Proposal," people in those churches that are
continuing to be biblical in their approach and continuing to rely on the Lord and His word will
scratch their heads and say, "What's so radical?
That's what we've been doing all along." We thank
God for those churches! Indeed our proposal would
not have been radical one hundred years ago. However, **because of the way psychological and
biblical counseling has swept into the church
and grabbed hold of minds and hearts, this
proposal is radical!** It will require a 180-degree
turn around for many Christians, pastors,
churches, Bible colleges, seminaries, and mission
boards. In fact, if the church or fellowship you
attend refers out to either psychological or biblical counselors or brings such individuals on staff,
we go so far as to say that you may need to find
one that has confidence in the Word of God beyond
giving lip service to it. That is **confidence
enough to trust mature believers in their
local church fellowship to minister to those**

suffering from problems of living, without biblical counseling manuals, workshops, seminars, degrees, or certificates. We hope and pray that our feeble efforts will encourage Christians to turn away from both psychology and the biblical counseling movement and to minister in the local body of believers as God has called them to do in His Word.

2

Psychotherapy (Talk Therapy)

Numerous Christians have followed the world in its infatuation with psychology. They have fallen for the same thing that Ellen Herman describes at the beginning of her book *The Romance of American Psychology*:

> Psychological insight is the creed of our time. In the name of enlightenment, experts promise help and faith, knowledge and comfort. They devise confident formulas for happy living and ambitious plans for dissolving the knots of conflict. Psychology, according to its boosters, possesses worthwhile answers to our most difficult personal questions and practical solutions for our most intractable social problems.
>
> In the late twentieth-century United States, we are likely to believe what psychological experts tell us. They speak with authority to a vast audience and have become familiar figures in most communities,

21

in the media, and in virtually every corner of popular culture. Their advice is a big business.[1]

Herman traces the rise of psychology as a helping profession and says:

> Throughout the entire postwar era, the United States has trained and employed more psychological experts, per capita, than any other country in the world. . . . Before World War II, professional healers and counselors were few; most individuals allied with psychology did work unrelated to "helping."[2]

Herman describes the omnipresence of psychology as having "seeped into virtually every facet of existence," but she says, "that does not mean that it has always been there or that what experts say has always mattered as much as it matters today."[3] Throughout her book, Herman reveals how "psychological help was defined so broadly that everyone needed it."[4] She concludes her review of the rise of psychology by asking a question: "Does the rise of psychology herald a new chapter in the evolution of humanism or merely indicate that Big Brother is bright enough to arrive cloaked in the rhetoric of enlightenment and health?"[5]

Psychological counseling theories and therapies are not only seeping into Christianity but are also staining the faith once delivered to the saints.

The rise of psychology in the church has heralded a new object of faith, one which for many people overshadows their faith in the promises of God, the sufficiency of His Word, the work of the Holy Spirit, and the life of Christ in the believer.

The Rise of Professional Therapists

With the rise of professional therapists during the past fifty years, pastors became convinced that they were not qualified to counsel the sheep. And, if the pastors, trained in the Word of God, were not qualified, how could the sheep themselves minister to the soul needs of one another? However, they faced a great dilemma, because most psychotherapists (psychological counselors) during the middle of the twentieth century were not Christians. Therefore, rather than looking to the Bible for answers, they decided that Christians should become trained in psychology so that they could minister to other Christians. Rather than solving the problem, however, they intensified it, because Christians taking these psychology courses were being trained in the ways of the world rather than in the Word of God. These therapies could only develop the flesh or the "old man." They were designed by unbelievers who had no real understanding of the difference between the flesh and the spirit, between the old man and the new man. Therefore all of these psychological systems of counseling were designed to fix and empower the very flesh that the Bible tells us to put off (Eph. 4:22).

Christians, noticing that there were some discrepancies between these psychological theories and the Bible, sought to solve that problem through integration, combining psychological theories and methods with biblical teachings. To do so, integrationists either adjusted the psychological theories to fit Scripture or adjusted Scripture to fit psychology. However, the latter seems to have won out, since Christians freely incorporate nearly all of the nearly 500 psychotherapies, many of which contradict each other. In looking at the contradictions among theories and therapies practiced, one can easily see that there is no controlling standard. Almost any psychological theory or method can become "biblicized" through adjusting Scripture to fit. Because of the heavy reliance on these secular theories, even attempts at integration will no doubt lead to strengthening the flesh rather than nourishing the spirit.

Neither the Bible nor research supports this move away from biblical ministry to psychological counseling. Rather than solving the problem of how to minister to the suffering soul, the church has:

(1) Abandoned the care of souls ministry.
(2) Sent the sheep elsewhere.
(3) Encouraged believers to train themselves in the ways of the world and "science falsely so-called" (1 Tim. 6:20).
(4) Embraced integration, which undermines and distorts Scripture.

(5) Brought psychological theories into the very heart of the church by employing paid therapists, by offering psychologically-based support groups, and by teaching the Bible from a psychological perspective.

Rather than seeing psychology through the lens of Scripture, most people now understand Scripture through the lens of psychology. That's how pervasive its influence has become, and it is one of the primary reasons why the church has become so worldly.

Now nearly every believer assumes that professional, psychologically trained Christians are the best people to help those with serious problems of living. Thousands of people have been trained as lay counselors, but the training has been conducted primarily by psychologically trained counselors. Therefore, even when there is personal ministry to one another, much of it is psychologically tainted. Moreover, these lay counselors are trained primarily in referring the difficult problems to professionals. And, to top it off, much of this psychological counseling (both professional and lay) is called "biblical counseling." Therefore, people who desire to follow God and His Word are duped into thinking they will receive ministry according to the Bible when they seek "biblical counseling." The situation is so grave that, aside from when we refer to the biblical counseling movement and to those who call themselves "biblical counselors," we generally avoid the expression "biblical counseling" when speaking about personal ministry to one another in the Body of Christ. That is because so much of what is labeled "biblical counseling" is tainted with unbiblical theories and therapies. We prefer the expressions "ministry," "biblical ministry" and "Christ-centered ministry."

How can the tide be turned? How can the church, which is racing headlong in one direction, be turned around? We have been attempting to warn believers of this downward spiral for over twenty-five years. Reasoning from the Bible has fallen on deaf ears. Facts have been ignored and very few see the tragedy of transferred trust: away from God and His Word, and solidly placed in fallible human opinions. Few see the tremendous wasteland of carnality where the flesh is nourished and the spirit is starved—all through trusting the wisdom of men and "science falsely so-called." We pray that God will open eyes and ears and renew the rightful functions of His Gifts and His Body.

Psychotherapy Not Much Relief

Why do Christians have faith in the promises of psychotherapy with its underlying psychologies? Obviously they believe it works. However, research reveals that it does not work as well as people think. Some years back the American Psychiatric Association (APA) Commission on Psychotherapies published a book titled *Psychotherapy Research: Methodological and Efficacy Issues.* In it the APA stated: "Whether the magnitude of the psychotherapy effect is medium or small remains a moot point; **no one has claimed that it is large**."[6] (Bold added.) While no researchers would claim that psychotherapy's level of relief is large, many practitioners and popularizers of psychology do.

Many new psychotherapies and research studies have occurred since the APA's findings, but the conclusion remains. In an interview with Dr. Martin Seligman, past president of the American Psychological Association, he was asked, "As a therapist and researcher who has spent three decades trying to build a bridge between the world of science and the world of everyday practice, are you impressed with the hard evidence of psychotherapy's effectiveness?" After discussing the results of averaging all the therapy outcome studies "which by now is in the four figures," Seligman admitted that "by and large, we produce only mild to moderate relief." After "regularly revising a formal textbook about abnormal psychology that has gone through five editions" over the past 25 years, Seligman indicated that not much has changed over the years with respect to his conclusion of "only mild to moderate relief" from psychotherapy.[7]

Seligman's "only mild to moderate relief" for psychotherapy may sound adequate. However, when factors such as the placebo effects and equal outcome effects for amateur helpers are considered, not much is left to the credit of psychological counselors or psychotherapists with their high fees, third-party payments, grandiose reputation, and expertise status in the courtroom. Christians need not be hoodwinked away from trusting God and His Word.

Placebo Effect

The placebo effect takes place when one has faith in a pill, person, process, or procedure, and it is this faith that brings about the healing. The pill, person, process, or procedure may all be fake, but the result is real. Notice what is working in the placebo. Faith! Why not encourage Christians to place their faith in God and His Word rather than in psychotherapists and their models and methods?

A group of researchers at Wesleyan University compared the benefits of psychotherapy with those of placebo treatments. The placebo treatments were activities (such as discussion of current events, group play reading, and listening to records) that attempted to help individuals without the use of psychotherapeutic techniques. The researchers concluded:

> . . . after about 500 outcome studies have been reviewed we are still not aware of a single convincing demonstration that the benefits of psychotherapy exceed those of placebos for real patients.[8]

Dr. Arthur Shapiro, clinical professor of psychiatry at Mount Sinai School of Medicine, suggests that the power of psychological counseling may be the effect of a placebo, which may explain the equal outcomes effect, which we will discuss in the next section. Shapiro says:

> Just as bloodletting was perhaps the massive placebo technique of the past, so psychoanalysis—and its dozens of psychotherapy offshoots—is the most used placebo of our time.[9]

Shapiro criticized his professional colleagues at an annual meeting of the American Psychopathological Association for ignoring placebo effects and therefore skewing the results of their research.[10] He believes that if placebo effects were considered, "there would be no difference between psychotherapy and placebo."[11]

Dr. Hans Eysenck, one of the best known psychologists in the world, said:

> The general tenor of the evidence produced in recent years seems to be that the conclusion of my 1952 article is still valid: psychotherapy works, as far as it does, by means of non-specific or placebo effects.[12]

The placebo not only affects the individual, but it affects those who come in contact with the individual. Everyone tends to feel and believe that progress will be made because something is being done. The placebo effect, along with other factors mentioned in this chapter, greatly diminishes the authority of any positive results reported for professional psychotherapy itself.

Equal Outcomes

The placebo effect may also be one reason for what researchers call "equal outcomes," which is the fact that all of the nearly 500 systems of psychotherapy appear to work equally well, regardless of their lack of compatibility with one another or even their contradictions. The *Handbook of Psychotherapy and Behavior Change* refers to the "general finding of no-difference in the outcome of therapy for clients who have participated in highly diverse therapies." The research literature repeatedly gives the following explanation: "Different therapies embody common factors that are curative although not emphasized by the theory of change central to a particular school."[13] These common factors would include the value of normal human interaction as well as the placebo effect. Thus the differences in the various psychotherapies are less important than the commonalities they share. And, these commonalities are extremely common, not the exclusive property of psychological counseling!

Dr. Joseph Wortis, State University of New York, reduces all the research down to its lowest common denominator. He says: "The proposition of whether psychotherapy can be beneficial can be reduced to its simplest terms of whether talk is very helpful." He goes on to say, "And that doesn't need to be researched. It is self evident that talk can be helpful." [14]

This equal outcomes result is also true in other areas of treatment. A newsletter from Harvard

University reports, "Alcoholism is notoriously the world's most serious drug problem."[15] A report in the *Journal of Studies on Alcohol* gives the equal outcomes result in the use of alcohol treatment programs. The National Institute on Alcohol Abuse and Alcoholism sponsored what has been called "one of the largest clinical experiments ever conducted." In comparing individuals in various programs (including those in hospital settings and those on the outside), none of the treatments were more successful than the others.[16]

Expectancy Arousal Hypothesis

Dr. David Shapiro has proposed an idea that would be a common factor for equal outcomes that could lead to success for therapies. He calls this idea the "expectancy arousal hypothesis," which he explains this way: "treatments differ in effectiveness only to the extent that they arouse in clients differing degrees of expectation of benefit."[17] According to this hypothesis, as the conversation or therapy proceeds and there is an arousal of positive expectancy in the client, then improvement will occur. Thus, according to Shapiro, as the therapist uses any one of a number of psychotherapies, the effectiveness will be related to the client's own expectancy of benefit. Therefore, the specific therapeutic conversation would not matter, but rather the client's expectancy of benefit. Any positive improvement has more to do with what the client brings to the therapy than with the therapy itself.

As the placebo depends on faith, the "expect-ancy arousal" is an expression of hope. Thus **faith and hope are the common and primary factors that contribute to positive outcomes in therapy**. Would it not be better for Christians to place their faith and hope in God and His Word than in the psychological wisdom of men and their systems of therapy? Can God be pleased with this misplaced faith and hope?

No Positive Evidence

As we have demonstrated elsewhere, there are both scientific and biblical reasons why psychol-ogy of this type should be rejected. We know from the research that the "training, credentials, and experience of psychotherapists are irrelevant"[18] and that "one's effectiveness as a therapist was unrelated to any professional training."[19] Based upon the equal outcomes results, as well as many other factors, Dr. Robyn Dawes, a widely recog-nized researcher, has summed it up very well by saying, "There is no *positive* evidence supporting the efficacy of professional psychology. There are anecdotes, there is plausibility, there are some common beliefs, yes—but there is no good evidence."[20] Dawes also provides research to demonstrate that the professional therapist's license protects the profession of psychotherapy rather than the consumer.

In an article titled "Psychological Warfare between Therapists and Scientists," Dr. Carol Tavris says:

The scientific illiteracy of psychotherapists has torn up families, sent innocent defendants to prison, cost people their jobs and custody of their children, and promoted worthless, even harmful therapies. A public unable to critically assess psychotherapists' claims and methods for scientific credibility will be vulnerable to whatever hysterical epidemic comes along next. And in our psychologically oriented culture, there will be many nexts. Some will be benign; some will merely cost money; and some will cost lives.[21]

We mention this information in passing and encourage you to read the evidence against psychotherapy and for the Bible in our earlier books. In addition to debunking the field of psychotherapy, we have also provided biblical reasons why Christians should not turn to the very wisdom of men about which God has warned us (1 Cor. 2).[22] The Bible is filled with a plethora of verses that show forth the origin of man, the condition of man, the salvation and sanctification of man, and the truth about mankind.

Psychotherapy is Not Science!

We have demonstrated elsewhere that psychotherapy does not qualify as a science. We have quoted eminent scholars in the field of psychology as well as philosophers of science to demonstrate that psychotherapy is not science. Dr. Sigmund Koch, Director of the National Science Foundation study resulting in a seven-volume series titled *Psychology: A Study of a Science*, said, "I think it by this time utterly and finally clear that *psychology cannot be a coherent science*."[23] (Italics in original.)

Dr. Karl Popper, one of the most outstanding philosophers of science during the twentieth century, considered that the psychological theories formulated by Freud, Adler, and others "though posing as sciences, had in fact more in common with primitive myths than with science; that they resembled astrology rather than astronomy."[24]

Psychological counseling theories are collections of human opinions arranged in theoretical frameworks. They are human inventions based on the perception and personal experiences of the theorists. These theories serve as a house of mirrors reflecting the theorists themselves. In her article "Theory as Self-Portrait and the Ideal of Objectivity," Dr. Linda Riebel clearly shows that "theories of human nature reflect the theorist's personality as he or she externalizes it or projects it onto humanity at large." She says that "the theory of human nature is a self-portrait of the theorist . . . emphasizing what the theorist needs" and that theories of personality and psychotherapy "cannot transcend the individual personality engaged in that act."[25]

Conclusion

Not one of the nearly 500 psychotherapy systems depends upon the knowledge of sin for their solutions or upon the understanding of repentance for relief. None of the biblical truths of salvation and sanctification are visible in the plethora of the often-conflicting psychological approaches. Instead, **these false psychological substitutes for the truth of Scripture minister to the flesh rather than to the spirit and steer people away from God and His Word**.

Counseling psychologies and psychotherapies have seduced the Body of Christ and can be found in almost every Bible college, seminary, Christian school, denomination, and church. Sometimes it appears in its undisguised form of Freudian, Adlerian, Jungian, etc. psychology, but most often it appears anonymously and too often disguised as gospel truth. While God has provided power in His Word, this type of psychology has so intimidated and captivated the church that it has become impotent in helping suffering saints in its midst.

Paul rightly warned the Colossians, "Beware lest any man spoil you through philosophy and vain deceit, after the tradition of men, after the rudiments of the world, and not after Christ" (Col. 2:8). These theories are various human philosophies about mankind. They are elaborate guesses and systems of belief built upon individual imagination. In fact, they represent a modern gnosticism with the idea that some people possess hidden knowledge of the soul. **Only God possesses the hidden knowledge of the soul, and He has revealed truth about the inner man in His Word.** Christians are foolish to look for this truth elsewhere and are warned against it. Paul determined not to use the "enticing words of man's wisdom . . . that your faith should not stand in the wisdom of men, but in the power of God" (1 Cor. 2:4-5). He did not want to have anything to do with the wisdom of the world (1 Cor. 2:6), because he knew the source of that wisdom is not God. We are admonished not to love the world or the things of the world (1 John 2:15), and one of the things of the world is its wisdom. The psychological counseling systems used by professing Christians were all invented by non-Christians, atheists, agnostics, occultists, and secular humanists.

The first step toward re-empowerment of God's people is to utterly reject this type of psychology with all of its false promises, premises, procedures, and pseudocures. Without a total rejection of this type of psychology, the church and God's people will remain powerless in the face of life's challenges and will yield to the confusion and contradictions of the plethora of talk therapies. If one will not outrightly reject such therapies, there is not much hope that one can move forward to the empowerment God provides. **Christians should know and affirm that such psychology is merely the hunches, opinions, guesses, and particularly the wisdom of men that God rejects (1 Cor. 2). They should step out in faith, depending solidly upon the Word of God and the work of the Holy Spirit.** The more Christians are intimidated by college degrees and training in psychology, the less likely they will be effective in helping fellow Christians in need. The less Christians are intimidated by college degrees and training in psychology, the more likely they will be effective in helping fellow believers.

We so often hear from Christians that they do not know what to do when confronted with a personal or interpersonal problem, whether it is an individual or a couple. Our goal is that Christians will abandon the myths of psychological counseling theories and methodologies and look to the Lord to enable them to minister. We want to convince believers that they are competent to minister in the Lord so that they will be confident to do so.

3

The Biblical Counseling Movement

When a number of Christians were alarmed at the way psychological counseling was over-running Christianity, they attempted to reverse the trend by substituting psychological counseling with biblical counseling. Indeed they were moving in the right direction—back to the Bible! However, the heavy influence of psychological counseling on the biblical counseling movement can be seen in biblical counseling leaders calling what they do "An alternative to secular psychology." Since when is the Bible just an alternative?

As the biblical counseling movement took hold, it began to reflect aspects of the psychological counseling model in a number of ways. One of the primary ways it replicated the world was to have trained counselors. In other words, there were to be special people who would be trained to do the counseling. This training was held up as essential if one were to minister to another person in need.

Training programs were established and in no time there was a division among believers between the elite—those who were trained and could therefore counsel a fellow believer—and the non-elite—those who were untrained and therefore "unqualified" to come alongside to minister to a fellow believer.

Historically the psychological counseling movement accelerated during post World War II years as Ellen Herman details in her book, which was mentioned earlier.[1] In the wake of its rise and seeming success and following it by about thirty years, the biblical counseling movement was spawned in the early seventies. To get a more accurate perspective on this issue, think back even thirty years. Where were the biblical counseling manuals, workshops, seminars, degrees, and certificates then? And now, if believers have not attended one of the above or obtained a degree or certificate from one of the above, they will neither feel prepared nor be trusted to "counsel" others.

Schools and seminaries set up classes, textbooks and manuals were written, and organizations were formed to certify biblical counselors. Before long there was a whole cadre of biblical counselors training more and more people in biblical counseling, and the leading trend was counseling. If anyone had a problem, the advice was, "You need counseling." Then those who were not helped by biblical counselors ended up going to psychological counselors, because faith in counseling had been firmly established among Christians. Therefore, rather than replacing psychological counselors, biblical counselors often became stepping stones to psychological counseling. With "Christian psychologists" the line of distinction became very blurry, since many psychologists refer to themselves as "biblical counselors" or "Christian counselors."

However, Christians do not need any of this counseling training. There is no evidence that lengthy training programs, certificates, practice counseling, or seminars will enable one Christian to minister more effectively than another. Exhaustive (and exhausting) manuals (as used in the biblical counseling movement) with numerous unnecessary details can actually serve to hinder people more than help them in ministering to another individual. Instead of approaching the ministry interaction by looking to see what the Lord will bring forth, their minds are often filled with trying to remember a similar case described in some manual and what verses were used there. Or, they just feel too intimidated by the fear that they have not taken enough courses and or studied their manuals sufficiently. **One purpose here, as in our other previous books and articles, is to convince Christians that they can effectively minister to fellow believers without having a college degree in psychology or being a licensed professional counselor or even having a Bible college or seminary degree or certificate in biblical counseling.**

Case Studies

Case studies are often used in psychology and biblical counseling, usually to show forth the efficacy of a particular idea or methodology. Aside from the use of brief examples to illustrate a point, we are opposed to the use of case studies for a variety of reasons.

Drs. Elizabeth Loftus and Melvin Guyer wrote a two-part article with the subtitle "The Hazards of the Single Case History." They began by saying:

> Case histories have a long and cherished tradition in science. They are compelling anecdotes, often powerful enough to generate entire theories of behavior. Freud built the edifice of psychoanalytic theory on the very few cases he saw in therapy. Bruno Bettelheim used a few cases of autistic children to conclude that autism is caused by "refrigerator" mothers. Psychiatrist Cornelia Wilbur's account of her patient, "Sybil," captivated millions of people who believed the story of Sybil's "multiple personalities."[2]

All of these theories, based on "very few cases," have been powerfully influential in the practice of psychotherapists; **but all have been debunked**. Loftus and Guyer say:

> But case studies, by definition, are bounded by the perceptions and interpretations of

the storyteller. If they are well told . . .
readers often find them far more persua-
sive and compelling than the stodgy
numbers and cautions of science.[3]

Dr. Paul Meehl, a past president of the American Psychological Association, once wrote an
extensive paper as to "Why I Do Not Attend Case
Conferences," in which he indicates a multitude
of reasons for his concerns.[4] Many biblical counselors use case studies throughout their books,
manuals, and conferences, and many of the same
objections apply. In one instance the biblical counselor used a case of a person whom he had never
met, but had only heard about from a third party.
Caution: while brief examples may be all right, do
not be intimidated by these biblical counseling
case histories that prove an approach or point of
view of the biblical counselor or are used to
demonstrate how to counsel, whether presented
in writing or given verbally at conferences.

It is time Christians give up trying to learn
how to counsel by studying or listening to case
histories. In addition to other reasons given above,
case histories can get in the way. Two people could
have exactly the same external problem, but only
God knows the specifics of what and how for a
particular person. This is why we say that those
who minister to one another need to get **in** the
way and **out of** the way. They need to be available, but they need to let God work rather than
push their own agenda.

The Myth of Specialized Training

This idea of needing specialized training is a myth! **Any person who can be used by the Holy Spirit to lead another to salvation or along the way of sanctification is competent to be used by God to minister to another without needing specialized biblical counseling training.** The myth of needing specialized training has intimidated Christians from following God's command to draw alongside fellow believers experiencing problems of living. First came the intimidation that a person cannot help a fellow believer unless psychologically trained. Next came the intimidation that Christians cannot really help unless they are trained in biblical counseling. And, the worst stated or implied intimidation is that you could harm a person if you are not trained. Even seminary graduates, if they did not major in biblical counseling often consider themselves "unqualified" to counsel. They may be able to pray, preach, and teach God's Word from the pulpit, but they are too intimidated to minister personally to the sheep. Moreover they usually will not trust ordinary believers to minister to their sheep. They either send them to psychologically trained counselors or to those who are trained in "biblical counseling."

As we demonstrated earlier, positive results from personal interactions labeled *psychotherapy* and *counseling* do not come from the specifics of theory or methodology. In fact, the counselor is not really the primary element of change in either psychological or biblical counseling. Too much attention, importance, and responsibility have been placed upon the human counselor as being the expert who brings about the change. As research has shown, change has more to do with the client or counselee than with the therapist or counselor; it also has more to do with the client or counselee than with the theory or methodology. In the Body of Christ, change has to do with the Lord working in His child. The one who draws alongside to minister, even in the most difficult situations, is but a shadow compared to the Lord and the one seeking help! Therefore, believers need not be intimidated when the Lord calls them to minister to one another, because in doing so they are serving the Lord in obedience, as He ministers to the individual and as the individual responds to the Lord.

Personal ministry to one another in the Body of Christ, when a brother or sister is suffering from problems of living, is often a shared ministry with the Lord working through a number of His children to assist the one in need. Moreover, as the Lord works, all have the opportunity to grow in the knowledge of God and in wisdom and spiritual understanding. Every believer involved in God's work benefits and grows!

The Number One Reason
Why People Change

In the previous chapter, we mentioned the equal outcomes that occur among the various psychotherapies as well as among other treatment programs such as those for alcoholism. The *Handbook of Psychotherapy and Behavior Change* makes it clear that client characteristics make a big difference with respect to outcomes in therapy. The *Handbook*'s "Summation" states:

> . . . it is the client more than the therapist who implements the change process. If the client does not absorb, utilize, and follow through on the facilitative efforts of the therapist, then nothing happens. Rather than argue over whether or not "therapy works," we could address ourselves to the question of whether or not "the client works"! [5]

Clients motivated to change who are therapized by a variety of therapies and therapists will certainly experience greater change than clients who do not really want to change.

The *Journal of Studies on Alcohol* says, with respect to equal outcomes in alcoholism treatment, the only differences in success had to do with other factors, such as personal motivation.[6] The Harvard newsletter makes it clearer yet by stating:

> Because Alcoholism, like all addictions, is a disorder of motivation, a full commitment to change is not only a cause of recovery but often the largest part of recovery itself. In a sense, all addiction treatments are ways of improving motivation.[7]

In the Foreword to *The Great Psychotherapy Debate*, Gene Glass says:

> The common factors position (namely, that all of the many specific types of psychotherapeutic treatment achieve virtually equal . . . benefits because of a common core of curative processes) can move the focus of psychotherapy training and theory itself from therapist to client, from how the therapist "cures" to how the client "heals." [8]

We conclude from all the research that the number one reason equal outcomes occur in various treatment programs is because of the clients rather than the therapists or the therapies. **The more motivated the individual, the more likely that change will occur. The less motivated the individual, the less likely that change will occur.** As we mentioned earlier, Christians do not need scientific research to demonstrate what the Bible already teaches, but it is interesting to note that the above research confirms what the Bible already declares about individual responsibility and motivation. However, in psychological and biblical counseling there is a great dependence on both the counselor and the process of counseling; whereas in Christ-centered ministry a seeker is encouraged to depend on the Lord. The less involvement of the helper, the better, and the more likely that spiritual growth will occur. Christ-centered ministry helpers must follow John the Baptist when he said, "He must increase, but I must decrease" (John 3:30).

Professionals versus Amateurs

The Lord is involved in the process of Christ-centered ministry as believers turn to Him and to His Word and encourage one another along the path of sanctification. Because the responsibility for change and growth is between the one seeking help and the Lord, believers need not fear drawing alongside to minister to one another if they have not been trained in psychological or biblical counseling. Furthermore, the research demonstrates that amateur counselors do as well as professionals.[9] It would be easy to provide a list of studies indicating the effectiveness of nonprofessional therapists. For example, the *Handbook of Psychotherapy and Behavior Change* reports:

> In a meta-analytic review of studies that address level of training, Berman and Norton concluded that professionally trained therapists had no systematic advantage over nonprofessional therapists in evoking treatment gains.[10]

Dr. Robyn Dawes says:

> Evaluating the efficacy of psychotherapy has led us to conclude that professional psychologists are no better psychotherapists than anyone else with minimal training—sometimes those without any training at all; the professionals are merely more expensive.[11]

The best possible test comparing professionals and nonprofessionals could not be conducted because it would involve deception. The best comparison would involve giving the nonprofessionals titles, degrees, credentials, etc., equivalent to the professionals. Eysenck makes a point about placebo treatments that usually involve amateurs and are used in comparison to professional psychotherapeutic treatment. He says:

> Nothing is said about the *quality* of the placebos used. To be effective, placebos should contain all the theoretically effective elements of the treatment that is being tested; that means equal duration, equal attention, and **equal belief in effectiveness on the part of the patient**. I have never seen a study that even approximated, let alone reached, such a degree of equivalence.[12] (Italics in original, bold added.)

The same criticism applies to the use of nonprofessionals. To overcome this criticism, we suggest that the professionals be stripped of their titles, degrees, credentials, etc. For a fair comparison, the therapy clients would not know the backgrounds of either the nonprofessionals or the professionals. The reason for this is obvious. If the professionals are presented with all of their titles, etc., they would have all the culturally sanctioned assets accruing to other professionals in our society. In other words, they will have a greater placebo effect.

One additional ingredient needed to create as much equivalency as possible is to use individuals from other people-oriented professions who have NOT been psychotherapeutically trained, but who have equal educational attainments in their own fields. For example, one could select engineers, biologists, physicists, chemists, and other such professionals to serve as the nonprofessional therapists.

We would like to see a similar experiment conducted between degreed or certificated individuals in biblical counseling and those who are in no way trained in biblical counseling. For a fair comparison, those who come for help would not know the backgrounds of either the trained or untrained biblical counselors. If all items are kept equal except for the biblical counseling training of the one group, we predict that the untrained group would do as well or better, unless the untrained group has bought into the intimidation.

An excellent example of how culturally-sanctioned assets influence the outcome can be seen in the following description of findings reported in *Psychotherapy Research: Methodological and Efficacy Issues*, published by the American Psychiatric Association:

> An experiment at the All-India Institute of Mental Health in Bangalore found that Western-trained psychiatrists and native healers had a comparable recovery rate. The most notable difference was that the so-called "witch doctors" released their patients sooner.[13]

A study of professional and nonprofessional therapists by researcher Dr. Hans Strupp at Vanderbilt University compared the mental-emotional improvement of two groups of male college students. Two groups of "therapists" were set up to provide two groups of students with "therapy." The two student groups were equated on the basis of mental-emotional distress as much as possible. The first group of therapists consisted of five psychiatrists and psychologists. "The five professional therapists participating in the study were selected on the basis of their reputation in the professional and academic community for clinical expertise. Their average length of experience was 23 years."

The second group of "therapists" consisted of seven college professors from a variety of fields, but without therapeutic training. Each untrained "therapist" used his own personal manner of care, and each trained therapist used his own brand of therapy. **The students seen by the professors showed as much improvement as those seen by the highly experienced and specially trained therapists.**[14] An important ingredient here is the fact that the professors, though amateurs at therapy, had the necessary culturally sanctioned assets equivalent to those of the professional therapists.[15]

Numerous other studies support the effectiveness of nonprofessionals. However, one aspect of most of these studies, which would put the amateurs at a disadvantage, is the placebo effect of the patient who knows that he is seeing a professional rather than an amateur. The expectation of cure, which does work as a placebo, is much higher when people think that professional experts are helping them rather than just regular persons. If this placebo effect were absent, we believe that the amateurs would actually do better than the professionals. Moreover, there would be greater eternal results among Christians if people truly trusted the Lord, obeyed His Word, and followed His instructions for ministering to one another (Gal. 6:1-2).

Counseling as Discipleship

Some biblical counselors claim to be discipling believers. Throughout the Gospels, the followers of Jesus were called "disciples." The word translated "teach" in Matthew 28:19 means "instruct," "teach," or "disciple" and can be translated "make disciples." When Jesus taught, He was making disciples—followers of Him and of His teachings. When Peter, Paul, and the other apostles preached and taught, they were teaching people to be disciples of Jesus. Preachers and teachers of God's Word are continuing to teach people to follow Christ. However, the modern-day idea of equating counseling with discipling can only apply to when the counselors are teaching people biblical truth and teaching them to follow Jesus. All the rest of what goes on in counseling, particularly the psychological methodology gleaned from the world and the central activity of talking about problems cannot be called discipleship.

Christ-centered ministry aims at making and encouraging disciples in the faith. However, over the past 35 years the word "discipling" has taken on baggage that Jesus never intended. Discipling became a relationship in which one person was the discipler (one-up) and the other was the disciple (one-down). In this relationship the disciplers often took a great deal of authority over the disciples to the point of telling them what to do and making their decisions. Counseling has certainly taken on some of this unbiblical form of discipling, as counselors (one-up) often exercise authority in their counselees' lives (one-down), as they often make decisions for them, and as they directly or indirectly tell them what to do. Quite often such counseling-discipling makes people disciples of their counselors. Christ-centered ministry works against such dependence and encourages people to be dependent on Christ rather than on another person. In fact, Christ-centered ministry works to free people to walk with Christ, to take their problems to Him instead of to other people, and to be so connected to the Body of Christ that they are both giving and receiving the life of Christ.

Conclusion

Believers need to learn to come to Christ in the time of need, because only through Christ will they find His will and His way in each situation. Every problem or trial is meant to conform us to the image of Christ. Thus every trial must be brought to Him, not to manipulate or to get one's own way, but to find out what God is doing and wants to do. Yes, there are pastors, teachers, and fellow believers who give wise counsel during times of need. However, one does not have to counsel or be counseled to find wisdom.

Personal ministry should be a natural part of the daily life of the church through the preaching and teaching of the Word and through believers praying for each other and encouraging, admonishing, exhorting, and confronting one another. **All this can be done without a system, center, or ministry of "biblical counseling."** Though the justifiers of biblical counseling may contend otherwise, all of this was done prior to the beginning of the biblical counseling movement only about thirty years ago, at least in churches that were preaching and teaching the whole counsel of God.

We, as well as others, have spoken out against the errors of the biblical counseling movement. No Christian counseling organization of which we are aware has severely criticized and refused membership to those biblical counselors who charge fees or encourage donations for their services; nor have these organizations excluded from membership those who have biblical counseling offices or centers outside the church. In addition, many of the well-known leaders of the biblical counseling movement are also members of organizations that are blatantly integrationist or outrightly psychological. These, as well as many other unbiblical practices, have led us not to recommend any of the various biblical counseling organizations.

We want to make it clear that, although we are opposed to the biblical counseling movement with its training and credentials, we are adamantly in favor of Christians studying the Bible and becoming well taught in the Word in their local congregations, without such teachings being bound to the biblical counseling movement. **The person who is saved and being sanctified through the trials of life is sufficient to be used by God in another person's life through the work of the Holy Spirit, but without biblical counseling training.**

One need not look up to biblical counselors, even those who are well-known through books, lectures, and organizations or who have been doing biblical counseling for years, as being better at ministering to a fellow believer in a local congregation than one who has found God sufficient through the trials of life and matured through obedience to His Word.

4

The Rise & Practice of Problem-Centered Counseling

God has given us great and precious promises in His Word. Christians have all they need in the Word to deal with problems of living. Yet, over the past fifty years there has been a dramatic shift in confidence on the part of Christians—away from God's Word and toward man's wisdom to deal with people's thinking, feeling, speaking, acting, and relating with one another.

This shift occurred because of psychology's rising popularity, first outside the church and then inside the church and its various institutions— Bible colleges, seminaries, Christian schools, and mission agencies. The type of psychology to which we refer is psychotherapy and its underlying psychologies. Beginning with Anton Mesmer and Sigmund Freud and then spreading to others, this leaven of psychology has now come to full loaf.

Thus far we have coauthored a number of books and articles, many of which have provided

biblical and scientific reasons to reject psychotherapy and much of what is called "biblical counseling."[1] However, as important as it is to expose
the fallacies and failures of psychological counseling, it is even more important to our present
concern that we reveal the source of problem-
centered counseling, which has become the standard form of counseling both outside and inside
the church.

Conversation as Cure, Rhetoric as Remedy

In his book *Mesmerism and the American Cure
of Souls,* Robert Fuller describes how mesmerism
promised great psychological and spiritual advantages. Its promises for self-improvement, spiritual
experience, and personal fulfillment were especially welcomed by unchurched individuals. Fuller
says that mesmerism offered "an entirely new and
eminently attractive arena for self-discovery—
their own psychological depths." He says that "its
theories and methods promised to restore individuals, even unchurched ones, into harmony with
the cosmic scheme."[2] Fuller's description of
mesmerism in America is an accurate portrayal
of twentieth-century psychotherapy as well as of
so-called mind-science religions. The goal and
impetus for discovering and developing human
potential grew out of mesmerism and stimulated
the growth and expansion of psychotherapy, positive thinking, the human potential movement, and
the mind-science religions.

In a section titled "Mesmerism: The Beginning
of American Psychology," the American Psychologi-

cal Association's book titled *History of Psychotherapy: A Century of Change* says:

> Historians have found several aspects of mesmerism and its offshoots that **set the stage for 20th-century psychotherapy.** It promoted ideas that are quintessentially American and have become permanent theoretical features of our 20th-century psychological landscape.[3] (Bold added.)

Mesmer's far reaching influence gave an early impetus to scientific-sounding religious alternatives to Christianity. And he started the trend of medicalizing religion into treatment and therapy. Nevertheless, he only gave the world false religion and false hope. Professor of psychiatry Thomas Szasz describes Mesmer's influence this way:

> Insofar as psychotherapy as a modern "medical technique " can be said to have a discoverer, Mesmer was that person. Mesmer stands in the same sort of relation to Freud and Jung as Columbus stands in relation to Thomas Jefferson and John Adams. Columbus stumbled onto a continent that the founding fathers subsequently transformed into the political entity known as the United States of America. Mesmer stumbled onto the literalized use of the leading scientific metaphor of his age for explaining and exorcising all manner of human problems and passions, a **rhetori-**

cal device that the founders of modern depth psychology subsequently transformed into the pseudomedical entity known as psychotherapy.[4] (Bold added.)

In his book *The Myth of Psychotherapy*, Szasz expands on his comment that Mesmer is really an early father of psychotherapy through his use of rhetoric. He says:

Trying to demonstrate that psychotherapy is rhetoric is like trying to demonstrate that the cow is a mammal. Why do it, then? For two reasons: because it is now the official opinion of the dominant institutions of society that psychotherapy is a form of medical treatment; and because an appreciation of rhetoric has all but disappeared from contemporary consciousness. Seeing psychotherapy as conversation rather than cure thus requires that we not only consider the error of classifying it as a medical intervention, but that we also look anew at the subject of rhetoric and assess its relevance to mental healing.

In plain language, what do patient and psychotherapist actually do? They speak and listen to each other. What do they speak about? Narrowly put, the patient speaks about himself, and the therapist speaks about the patient. In a broader sense, however, both also speak about other persons and about various matters of concern to their lives. The point is that each tries to move the other to see or do things in a certain way. That is what qualifies their actions as fundamentally rhetorical. If the psychotherapist and his patient were not rhetoricians, they could not engage in the activity we now conventionally call *psychotherapy*—just as if cows did not suckle their young, we could not call them mammals.[5]

Thus psychotherapy has Mesmeric and Freudian origins, and, though it has gone through up to almost 500 varieties, it still exists essentially as rhetoric as remedy and conversation as cure.

This rhetoric as remedy and conversation as cure became professionalized and placed in the hands of these new (at the time) practitioners. Those who followed eventually needed to become educated and licensed. It was a milestone in the history of psychology and now this talk therapy has been fully accepted in both the world and the church. These sorcerers of the soul now set the standards for solutions of the soul—solutions that have not only been wholeheartedly embraced but also practiced and expected in the church. **The activity of conversation as cure or rhetoric as remedy is promulgated through problem-centered counseling, which is the standard outside and inside the church; it is the standard in both psychological and biblical counseling.** A return to the true biblical way will be difficult to accomplish, but a drastic turnaround is necessary if spiritual growth is the goal rather than fleshly change.

Problem-Centered Counseling

A major difference between what both psychologists and many of those who are called biblical counselors do and what we recommend is in response to problems of living. The problem-centered counselor finds out what the problem is through conversation with the client. The client describes the problem in as much detail as possible and the therapist proposes a methodology for a solution. Even Christian licensed psychotherapists, if reimbursed by insurance, must practice according to their licenses. Thus, there is little, if any, mention of sin, repentance, salvation, and sanctification, to mention just a few biblical doctrines. The focus must be on the client, not on the Lord Jesus Christ. In essence, psychological counselors aim at changing thinking, feeling, or behaving by psychological methodology. However, problems of living with their effects on the client are the focus of the various methodologies.

Irwin Kutash and Alexander Wolf's *Psychotherapist's Casebook: Theory and Technique in the Practice of Modern Therapies* was written to "demonstrate, through annotated case histories, the major therapy techniques in present use."[6] Kutash and Wolf state: "In all approaches, the psychological issues of the client constitute, in one way or another, the main focus."[7] The client (i.e., the self) comes with a problem. The counseling is directed at the self with the problem. Thus, problem centered counseling is actually self-centered counseling. The two are inextricably linked. **It**

would be appropriate to refer to the activity as problem/self-centered counseling.
One of the biggest shortcomings of biblical counseling is that it too often reflects the psychotherapeutic standard of problem-centeredness. In attempting to minister to the same issues treated by psychological counseling, biblical counselors often pay more attention to the personal or relational problems than to the individual's relationship to the Lord and the process of sanctification. Problem-centered counseling often occurs in two forms. One is behaviorism and the other is seeking insight into the inner man. Therefore, Biblical counselors either attempt to solve problems at the surface level or they attempt to discover something about the inner man through various methods of exploration. The possible dangers are superficiality, legalism, and formulas on the one hand, or attempting to analyze the soul or the idols of the heart on the other.

Behaviorism: Working on the Outside

Those problem-centered biblical counselors who attempt to change behavior often follow a works-oriented, unbiblical psychological behaviorism where the focus is on overt behavior and the removal or change in overt symptoms. In other words, they attempt to transform a person from the outside-in. They work on behavior with the idea that change in external behavior will result in internal right feelings, attitudes, and spiritual change. They say, "If you do right, you will feel right" and cite Genesis 4:4-7 as a biblical justification for working from the outside-in.

> And Abel, he also brought of the firstlings of his flock and of the fat thereof. And the LORD had respect unto Abel and to his offering: But unto Cain and to his offering he had not respect. And Cain was very wroth, and his countenance fell. And the LORD said unto Cain, Why art thou wroth? and why is thy countenance fallen? If thou doest well, shalt thou not be accepted? and if thou doest not well, sin lieth at the door. And unto thee shall be his desire, and thou shalt rule over him (Gen. 4:4-7).

By using a particular translation of Genesis 4:7 one might think that God is saying that Cain's countenance will be "lifted up." While the verse may well be translated "lifted up," there is nowhere else in Scripture where it is used in reference to feelings and attitudes. It has to do with being lifted up to a place of acceptance. God is not talking about Cain's feelings being lifted up. He is really talking about Cain being accepted in the same way that Abel was with his offering, if Cain would do the right thing. From the rest of Scripture doing the right thing would be more than an external act.

While God gives us instructions to obey, whether we feel like it or not, He does not guarantee that right feelings will follow or that inner, spiritual change will necessarily happen. Scripture does not present outward conformity to what is right as being sufficient or as being a way to change the inner man. Jesus, chastised the Pharisees:

> Woe unto you, scribes and Pharisees, hypocrites! for ye are like unto whited sepulchres, which indeed appear beautiful outward, but are within full of dead men's bones, and of all uncleanness. Even so ye also outwardly appear righteous unto men, but within ye are full of hypocrisy and iniquity (Matt. 23:27,28).

If any group could be used to demonstrate whether or not outward change produces inner change, the Pharisees would be the ones.

In both salvation and sanctification God is working on the inside and there is an inner response of faith, which precedes external change.

> For by grace are ye saved through faith; and that not of yourselves: it is the gift of God: not of works, lest any man should boast. For we are his workmanship, created in Christ Jesus unto good works, which God hath before ordained that we should walk in them" (Eph. 2:8-10).

Yes, there is to be outer change, but that change is wrought first on the inside by grace through faith. The story of Job demonstrates that God works to perfect and refine the inner man. Job is described as "perfect and upright, and one that feared God, and eschewed evil" (Job 1:1). Did he need change in his outward behavior? How might problem-centered counselors have dealt with Him? We see vivid examples of problem-centeredness in his first three friends. In contrast, God confronted the core of Job's being.

Working from the outside in can be reduced to a works-oriented behaviorism. One may indeed improve behavior, but, unless there is inner change, the outward conformity can simply be a work of the flesh. Biblical counselors may argue that Paul was problem-centered when he listed specific sinful behaviors and when he directed believers to change. However, when the Apostle Paul urges believers to put off specific sinful behaviors, such as in Colossians 3:8-10 and Ephesians 4:25-31, he is not isolating them from their source—the "old man" or the flesh. He is identifying behaviors that are indeed outward expressions of the inner man.

If a problem-centered counselor works on changing one particular behavior, the flesh may cooperate and be thereby strengthened. After all, unbelievers may not individually exhibit all the works of the flesh in their outward behavior. For instance, if the problem is anger, one may do all kinds of things to control the anger for personal benefit. Christ-centered ministry aims much higher, that is, putting off the "old man," being renewed in the mind (having a change of heart and direction), and putting on the new life in Christ. The flesh is willing to change certain behaviors. However, the issue is this: who is in charge? The Lord Jesus Christ or the fleshly self?

Working on the Inside

A second way that problem-centered biblical counselors attempt to bring about change reflects various forms of insight therapy, in which the counselor attempts to know what is on the inside that is driving present feelings and behavior. Some biblical counselors seek to identify idols of the heart. Indeed, they are looking for change in the right place, on the inside. However, when humans attempt to look inside another person they enter a guessing game. They connect certain outward expressions of behavior with certain "idols of the heart" and then attempt to help individuals confront their particular idols of the heart. However, this is like insight therapy—searching the inner man by looking at the outside and guessing about what is on the inside. Instead of moving the person closer to the Lord for Him to work on the inside, they try to help the person by giving their own ideas (guesses based on their own perceptions) as to what is going on inside.

Only the Lord can see inside a person. His Word declares. "The heart is deceitful above all things, and desperately wicked: who can know it? I the LORD search the heart, I try the reins, even to give every man according to his ways, and according to the fruit of his doings" (Jer. 17:9-10).

Even worse than looking for idols of the heart is what is known as "inner healing" in its various forms. Inner healing centers attention on both present and past problems, teaches that present problems are determined by past problems, and leads the individual into re-experiencing problems

from the distant past that may or may not have
occurred. Inner healing relies on suggestion and
memories that are faulty.[8] In addition to looking
for remote memories lurking beneath present
problems, some counselors look for demons infest-
ing believers. They give these so-called demons
names, conduct a ritual of casting them out, and
leave victims wondering if they are still infested
the next time they do what was supposedly caused
by a particular demon. Needless to say, people can
get into deep spiritual trouble with these forms of
problem-centered counseling. They are left floun-
dering in their flesh and dependent on the counselor to take them through more inner healing or
deliverance rituals.

While the Bible instructs believers as to what
to do and what not to do, it is not made up of prob-
lem-solving formulas. The Bible provides the
direction and means of change, but not in detailed
specifics of how this is to be accomplished in each
individual. That is because the Lord works
personally inside each one of His children through
the Holy Spirit, who works the details of change
in perfect wisdom and timing. If one could follow
formulas for change, people would end up trying
to work out their own sanctification apart from
God working inside them. If people could simply
follow formulas, there would be an independence
that goes against the entire thrust of the unique
relationship between the Lord and each believer,
as Jesus described in John 15. Without Him,
believers "can do nothing" (John 15:5).

God works the change on the inside and
enables believers to respond both internally and

externally in their behavior. "Wherefore, my beloved, as ye have always obeyed, not as in my presence only, but now much more in my absence, work out your own salvation with fear and trembling. For it is God which worketh in you both to will and to do of his good pleasure" (Phil. 2:12,13). The Word tells believers what they should do and the Holy Spirit enables them to do so. Because sanctification is a long process and because the sequence of change may be different in each individual, people try to speed up what they want to change through various human means, which actually put people into a cycle whereby they are back again striving in the flesh.

Looking at Problems or Beholding the Lord

Instead of focusing on problems or attempting to expose the heart, a pastor and his congregation should be involved in active sanctification, growing in the fruit of the Spirit, learning to walk according to the Spirit, with Jesus being the center of attention and becoming like Him the goal. While this is surely part of the ministry of individuals who call themselves biblical counselors, too much biblical counseling has become something in addition to sound doctrine and practice. The Bible reveals spiritual issues that underlie behavior. Thus it is entirely unnecessary and unscriptural to use psychological techniques or some biblical-sounding human means to gain insight into the inner man or to expose the heart and motivation, which is the work of the Holy Spirit.

Problem-centered counseling rests on the notion that once problems of living are solved spiritual growth will occur. However, rather than problems being the barrier to spiritual growth, spiritual stagnation is one reason for problems and can certainly be a barrier to solving them. Problems of living can actually serve as catalysts for spiritual growth. Therefore, the emphasis in Scripture is not on problem solving but rather on obeying the Lord, growing spiritually, and learning to walk according to the Spirit through the trials of life.

Trials responded to in the Lord can result in greater dependence on the Lord, greater love for God and one another, and an abundance of the fruit of the spirit, especially patience and long-suffering. Problem-centered counseling, on the other hand, can serve to postpone spiritual growth. It can keep people enmeshed in their woes and further exacerbate relational problems as they focus on and talk about the shortcomings of others.

It is a well-known fact that counselees often lie to their counselors. They lie for a variety of reasons, such as: embarrassment if the truth were known; to make themselves look good; to cover up illegal, immoral, or carnal activities; to condemn others or situations without fear of having to prove anything; or to relieve guilt. Even when counselees are attempting to be truthful, they do see situations from their own perspective. Therefore what they believe to be true may be incongruent with reality. Therefore, problem-centered counseling often involves what can only be labeled as "gossip" when the counselee talks about situations and people who are not present. In doing so, the counselee gives his own perception of the individuals and circumstances. The counselor generally believes what is said unless someone is there to present another side. As details are given the counselor is drawn into seeing other people and the situation from the counselee's viewpoint.

Since problem-centered counseling deals directly with the problems, details seem to be a necessary ingredient to solving or relieving them. Christ-centered ministry does not need such detailed information about the people involved in a person's problems because the direction of ministry is towards the Lord rather than into the problem. God knows exactly what is going on in the person's life and is able to guide and direct His children. Therefore the helper does not need to know the details (often gossip) about persons and problems that do not need to be known and are generally unverifiable. Because the direction of Christ-centered ministry is to draw close to the Lord, it is both possible and desirable for the helper to know little or nothing about the seeker's problems in order to be of help.

Rather than looking at their problems, believers would do well to look to the Lord and increase their knowledge of Him. "But we all, with open face beholding as in a glass the glory of the Lord, are changed into the same image from glory to glory, even as by the Spirit of the Lord" (2 Corinthians 3:18). The Lord changes the heart as people draw close to Him, study Him, and desire to grow like Him. Yes, they are to respond to God's work in them both on the inside and in outer behavior as God is working on the inside (Phil. 2:12,13). "The just shall live by faith" (Rom. 1:17), and faith is an inside response to God that shows up in obedience and in the good works that follow salvation (Eph. 2:10). **The less problem-centered the ministry, the more likely that spiritual change will occur.**

Counseling versus Ministry

The terms *counselor*, *counselee*, and *counseling* have such a strong hold on the biblical counseling movement that, if they were replaced by three other words, the movement would suffer irreparable damage. Why? Because of the power and status of those terms and the admiration of and trust in the practitioners. The power and prestige of the practitioners have drawn many into the movement.

As mentioned earlier, we prefer to use terms such as *helper, servant, seeker, fellow believer, ministry*, and *mutual care* when speaking of people meeting together regarding the issues of life and faith. Helps are among the gifts God has given the church: "And God hath set some in the church, first apostles, secondarily prophets, thirdly teachers, after that miracles, then gifts of healings, helps, governments, diversities of tongues" (1 Cor. 12:28). Helps are listed with the other ministries of the church, but *counselor* and *counseling* are not. In the Greek, the word *helps* "refers to rendering assistance, perhaps especially of help ministered to the weak and needy."[9]

Now, if biblical counselors were no longer to use the counseling words with all their power, prestige, and baggage and refer to themselves as biblical helpers, how many people would be desirous of filling that role? Consider the word *minister*, which in the Greek means, among other things, servant and menial.[10] How many biblical counselors would want to use the phrase "biblical minister" in the sense of being a servant and menially waiting on those in need?

Counselor, *counselee*, and *counseling* are not the best terms to use when Christians are ministering to one another in the Body of Christ. These terms are already pre-opted, co-opted, and post-opted by problem-centered counselors and the secular society that surrounds us. Use these terms and Christians will usually expect the counselors to solve problems, rather than themselves responding in faith and obedience to God's Word and His work in their lives. The word *counseling*, as in problem-centered counseling, carries too much baggage and gives certain implications of expertise and one-up-man-ship that detract from what should really be happening when two or more believers meet in God's presence to seek His wisdom and power for change in one's life or circumstances. Moreover, counseling, like psychotherapy, has all the weaknesses we have referred to in our book *Against "Biblical Counseling": For the Bible* (Chapter 4).

Accompanying the rise of problem-centered counseling is what we refer to as the "onerous ones."[11] (See Chapter 7.) Too many biblical counselors function like their psychological counterparts by developing a one-to-one, one-day-a-week, one-fifty-minute-hour, one-week-after-another, one-fixed-price, one-right-after-another, one-up/one-down relationship.[12] These onerous ones of problem-centered counseling set up an artificial relationship between two people, with one person being the needy one and the other person the so-called expert. In this one-up/one-down relationship, the needy one must bare his soul to the expert, who is supposed to figure it all out and solve the problem or facilitate change in the needy one. This relationship easily deteriorates to one of dependence, with the needy one dependent on the expert and the expert dependent on the needy one's money (if there is a fee for service).

While not all biblical counselors charge a fee, many do, especially if they are separated-from-the-church businesses. These biblical counselors are not doing anything that an ordinary Christian, in whom Christ lives and rules and who personally knows and applies God's Word, can't do. Ministry is required, not problem-centered counseling expertise. Therefore, there is no reason for anyone to charge fees for such ministry. If the price has already been paid by the blood of Jesus, why should there be a fee? In fact, we have called such charging money for ministry a form of Simony.[13] Some biblical counselors who have been trained in psychology or have obtained state counseling licenses go so far as to participate in third-party insurance reimbursement plans, which necessitates using practices within their license, such as mental-health designations for reimbursement, psychological diagnoses, and write-ups for continued counseling. Those who do that must be practicing psychology or they are being dishonest in their practice.

In addition to those onerous ones is the use of intake forms (like psychologists use) and personality tests, which are often used by problem-centered counselors and are usually worthless and misleading.[14] And, worst of all is the expectation that the counselor and the process of counseling will bring about the resolution of the problems—the shift in responsibility from the person to the counselor. All true Christians have the Holy Spirit living in them and are thereby enabled to obey God. They are responsible to God. They cannot obey God by shifting the responsibility to someone else.

The image of counseling is two or more people conversing, primarily about problems. One is the so-called expert and the other is the one with the problems. The sole activity is conversation. That is why it is often referred to as "talk therapy." In other words, the participants are communicating with each other with their voices and their ears. However, mutual care in the Body of Christ is not limited to talking. In addition to engaging the voice and the ears, Christ-centered ministry may necessarily involve using the hands, feet, and goods in ministering to a person in need. Besides verbal encouragement, a woman experiencing what is now labeled "postpartum depression" could also be helped with a few weeks of meals provided by members of the fellowship, some child care if there are older siblings, and even help with housework and shopping.

Another example may be of a woman whose husband has left her with three children. Besides encouragement and hope, she might need help caring for the children, paying the rent, and supplying food and clothing for her family. Christians need to heed James' admonition:

> If a brother or sister be naked, and desti-
> tute of daily food, And one of you say unto
> them, Depart in peace, be ye warmed and
> filled; notwithstanding ye give them not
> those things which are needful to the body;
> what doth it profit? (James 2:15-16).

The principle behind this verse may be applied in any number of situations in a local fellowship. How many counselors leave their clients with a comforting word, "Depart in peace, be ye warmed and filled," without extending themselves to meet a real need? Obviously, for James, such counseling talk would be a waste of time.

And, indeed, talk is often all that happens. People come to have their problems solved for them and figure that going to counseling is all they need to do besides paying the counselor's fee. There is often a false assumption that talking about a problem will make it go away. A person may feel better after having talked about the problem, but generally talk is not enough. There must be doing on the part of those involved in the conversation.

An additional problem arises now with using the words *counselor* and *counseling*. In certain States, using the words *counselor* or *counseling*, when referring to those believers who minister to one another in mutual care in the Body of Christ, would conflict with laws having to do with services offered to the public, whether inside or outside a church and either with or without a fee. Too often those who actually practice psychotherapy call what they do "biblical counseling" even though their practice involves more from secular theories and therapies than from the Bible.

Christians do NOT need problem-centered counseling! At times they may need help, advice, counsel, encouragement, support, assurance, fellowship, and personal ministry. They may need someone to draw alongside to confront, admonish, exhort, or remind them of the truth of God's Word. We all need instruction in God's Word. But, **no one needs psychological or biblical counseling as it is generally practiced today!** As we have demonstrated elsewhere, no such ministry of what today is called "biblical counseling" exists in the Bible; neither is there any example in the Bible that comes close to the biblical counseling movement as it exists today.[15]

Counseling often takes the place of personal responsibility and personal relationships. People often relate more with the counselor than with friends or family members. Moreover, people in counseling often develop dependence on the counselor rather than on the Lord. We still say that, at best, professional counselors are paid friends. Even if biblical counselors are free, the relationship of counseling can become artificial with the onerous ones and with the attention centered on the counselee and the problem. And, to continue the relationship, the counselee must continue to have problems.

What Can Be Done?

If Christians do not need specialized training in either psychotherapy (psychological counseling) or even biblical counseling and if they are not going to be problem-centered, who is qualified and how can they truly minister to fellow believers who are experiencing various problems of living? **Remember, anyone who can be used by the Holy Spirit to lead another to salvation or along the way of sanctification is competent to be used by God to draw alongside and minister to a fellow believer by grace through faith.**

5

Christ-Centered Ministry or Problem-Centered Counseling?

The usual process of counseling begins and ends with the counselee and his problems. The counselee comes to the counselor seeking relief and resolution. Counselees generally expect counselors to use their expertise to understand, reveal, and fix their problems. The counselor attempts to analyze the person and the problems and to bring help. If the counselor believes the counselee needs to change, he will attempt to bring about the change through conversation with or without assigned activities. However, the Bible shows a different way. **In Christ-centered ministry, relationship is given priority over problems.** Rather than attempting to facilitate change, the helper encourages the person seeking help to draw close to the Lord, because spiritual change and growth come

from the interaction between that person and the
Lord.

**Talking about problems should not be the
central content of personal ministry in the
Body of Christ. Problems should be seen as
opportunities for drawing close to the Lord
and growing spiritually.** We are not saying, "Do
not talk about problems!" This is not an either-or
situation; it is a matter of where the emphasis lies
and how problems are addressed and used to
motivate a believer to turn to the Lord, follow Him,
and be further transformed into the likeness of
Christ. **We are advising believers to minimize
and generalize talking about problems and
maximize and specialize in using problems
as reminders to draw one closer to God.** Pre-
occupation with problems and seeking solutions
through counseling often inhibit spiritual growth.
Put simply, Christ must be the center of Christ-
centered ministry whereas problems tend to be
the center of problem-centered counseling.

We know that considerable research dealing
with what is called "Post-Traumatic Stress Disor-
der" (PTSD) indicates that those who receive treatment "do no better than those who don't and that
a significant number of people treated . . . do even
worse than those who didn't receive treatment."
Reporting on the extensive research, the writer
says:

> This negative reaction seems to emerge
> because, for some people, the very act of
> focusing on their negative feelings . . . in-
> creases their distress and leads to more

difficulties, such as flashbacks, nightmares, and anxiety attacks.[1]

Using this as a hint, is it not possible that talking about problems, as in problem-centered counseling, is detrimental to those who seek relief by rehearsing, rehashing, reliving and regurgitating their problems? While most problem-centered counseling does not deal with PTSD, most counseling does involve "the very act of focusing on . . . negative feelings." This research conclusion about PTSD should by extension raise questions about problem-centered counseling.

As we said earlier, problem-centered counseling was established by such men as Mesmer and Freud and popularized by their followers. They set the standard for counseling. In fact most Christians who seek counseling are expecting to have their problems solved. Their goal is not spiritual growth, but problem resolution, because they see their problems as either unrelated to spiritual growth or hindrances to their spiritual well-being. But, which must come first? New life in Christ and learning to walk according to the Spirit or having problems of living fixed so that a person can hear the Gospel? Many counselors go so far as to say that a person cannot know God and grow in sanctification until the problems of living, especially the "hurts of the past," are dealt with. But that notion contradicts the Gospel of Jesus Christ and was not even considered necessary until the intrusion of extra-biblical ideas and the rise of psychological counseling. Jesus' death on the cross was sufficient to deal with the "hurts" and sins of the past and to generate and grow the new life in the believer.

Problem-centered talk therapy has become so firmly established that even biblical counselors focus on problems of living, even though there is a dramatic contrast between focusing on the person and his problems and emphasizing Christ and His life in the believer. Biblical ministry should help a person learn to walk with the Lord through problems, grow spiritually, and learn to trust Him for help. Biblical counseling can use the Bible cognitively and behaviorally, but unless it stimulates an inner experience of Christ's reality, presence, and activity, it can become legalistic and works oriented and lead to self-righteousness.

After a person is born again by grace through faith in the finished work of Jesus Christ, the Holy Spirit comes to live inside the person. Just as salvation is an inner work so also is sanctification, which works from the inside out with the Holy Spirit motivating change and growth according to the Word of God. In this process, problems of living are often used by God to convert sinners, motivate spiritual growth (Psalm 51), mold believers into the image of Christ (Romans 8:28,29), and even validate their connection with Christ and their service to Him (John 15:18,19).

Preaching, teaching, and living the Word of God have been the Lord's ways of initially converting and then guiding and growing His children, but **the whole idea of counseling during the last century has shifted the focus away from God to self and away from salvation and sanctification to problem solving**.

While many biblical counselors may also be teaching and living the Christian life during counseling, too much time and effort are spent working directly on problems. This problem-centered approach is common among biblical counselors.

People who turn to counselors to solve their problems often keep coming back, because as soon as one problem is addressed or partly resolved another problem pops up. The person becomes dependent on the counselor to solve his problems and tell him what to do. The more a person looks to another person to solve problems of living, the more likely he will be to take subsequent problems to the counselor and thereby become impotent in dealing with his own problems of living.

Spiritual Growth

Christians need to return to the way the Lord has delineated in Scripture—utilizing the doctrines of salvation and sanctification for spiritual growth—for purposes much higher than solving people's problems. God's purpose is to form each believer into the image of Christ. Paul's goal was to present every believer perfect (complete) in Christ. As one grows spiritually and draws closer to God there will be a greater desire to please Him through obedience and greater wisdom to do so. In biblical ministry the encouragement is there for the person to be growing in Christ (putting off the old, putting on the new, and walking according to the Spirit). From this position people will be better equipped to take responsibility for their own lives, handle problems of living, and begin to help others.

The walk of faith is to be like salvation— received by grace through faith—in that each subsequent step of the believer is in relationship to the risen Christ and lived by grace through faith.

> As ye have therefore received Christ Jesus the Lord, so walk ye in him: Rooted and built up in him, and stablished in the faith, as ye have been taught, abounding therein with thanksgiving" (Col. 2:6,7).

Christians are God's workmanship from beginning to end (Eph. 2:8-10). Jesus is "the author and finisher of our faith" (Heb. 12:2). "The just shall live by faith" (Romans 1:17). During sanctification God does the main work and the believer responds by grace through faith. As the Holy Spirit works the Word of God into believers, they grow in love for God, in humility, and in submission to the Spirit. This does not mean that the person does not do anything, but that the spiritual life is truly of the Lord and the believer's involvement is enabled by the Holy Spirit. Biblical counseling that directly attempts to change behavior can easily resemble a works-oriented sanctification. Yes, there is to be obedience, but that obedience is to be a response of faith to the presence, truth, and work of Christ.

Experiencing the Life of Christ

Christ-centered ministry attempts to encourage living and experiencing the life of Christ in the believer. Thus greater attention needs to be given to those sections of Scripture that talk about the intimate relationship of Christ and the believer. This intimacy is not a warm, fuzzy feeling but rather the realization of the reality of the oneness Jesus referred to in His prayer to His Father on the night of His betrayal.

> Neither pray I for these alone, but for them also which shall believe on me through their word; that they all may be one; as thou, Father, art in me, and I in thee, that they also may be one in us: that the world may believe that thou hast sent me. And the glory which thou gavest me I have given them; that they may be one, even as we are one: I in them, and thou in me, that they may be made perfect in one; and that the world may know that thou hast sent me, and hast loved them, as thou hast loved me (John 17:20-23).

Christ-centered ministry encourages a personal experience of the reality of God's Word. Therefore the experience must be according to the Word and not according to the flesh. One must stay within biblical restraints. An experience of spiritual reality does not have to be emotional. It can be cognitive awareness of truth—a realization

of an aspect of God or of His Word. It is like a surge
of light and life within the soul. The Spirit of God
penetrates the soul with truth and grace: the truth
to follow by grace through faith. When contem-
plating the glory of God and His intimate
relationship with each of His children, a realization of majesty and a sense of awe overwhelm the
soul and the response is worship, praise, adora-
tion, and obedience.

Preaching, teaching, singing, praising,
worshipping, and serving God should point to Him,
bring the person closer to Him, and reveal Him in
such a way as to touch the mind and emotions
and to affect behavior. The sermons and songs
must be life giving in presenting truth and reflecting Christ. And, the believer must attend to the
message in word and song with an expectancy to
receive from God and a readiness to respond in
faith and obedience.

We are not recommending that people should
look for a particular type of experience. They are
to look for Christ in the Word and in every situation of life. At all times there needs to be an awareness of His presence, power, and love, an expectation for Him to be at work in the believer, and an
active waiting. All must be done within the context
of Scripture so that one does not stray into legalism on the one hand or unbiblical emotionalism
on the other. "For the law was given by Moses, but
grace and truth came by Jesus Christ" (John 1:17).
Grace—all that Christ gives the person—is truth
experienced. We have both the written Word and
the living Word. The written Word serves as a standard by which we can gauge whether or not what

we are experiencing is the living Word or our own (or someone else's) imagination.

Christ-centered ministry aims at Christians growing in experiential knowledge of Christ. Such knowledge is more than knowing about Him and even beyond what we gain from reading the Bible. We know Him experientially as He reveals His truth and will to us and as we respond in faith and obedience. Through knowing Him believers are truly changed from the inside-out. This is why all ministry must be Christ-centered because we must know Him in order to become like Him.

> Now the Lord is that Spirit: and where the Spirit of the Lord is, there is liberty. But we all, with open face beholding as in a glass the glory of the Lord, are changed into the same image from glory to glory, even as by the Spirit of the Lord (2 Cor. 3:17,18)

Believers are not under the law or under some kind of legalism. If the Spirit of the Lord is in them they are free from the law of sin and death. They are free to grow in Christ. Believers are transformed by paying attention to all that Christ is and comprehending the majesty of His person, perfection, and present glory as the risen Lord, who is "before all things, and by Him all things consist" (Col. 1:17). Therefore, instead of giving primary attention to self and circumstances— where they may be stuck—believers need to turn their attention to Christ. This is the way of holiness, sanctification, and ongoing spiritual growth.

While we can bring forth Scriptures to encourage people to grow in this experiential knowledge of Christ, only the Holy Spirit can quicken the mind and heart and only the individual person can respond. There is no human mediator between Christ and the believer to make this happen. One should not try to make it happen through mood altering techniques, such as certain kinds of music or prescribed meditations designed to bring about a supernatural experience. We are not encouraging mysticism, but rather spiritual reality. Beware of highly emotional experiences that center on oneself or one's own past, which would very likely lead to energizing the flesh rather than to experiencing God in His truth and glory.

The Word of God beautifully and in a perfectly balanced manner appeals to the mind, emotions, and will. God created humans with cognitive and affective qualities: both mind and emotions. One without the other can lead to legalism in one extreme direction and emotionalism in the other extreme direction—a rigidity in one direction and a lack of restraint in the other. One of the enormous problems with academically studying the Bible as in Bible colleges and seminaries is that the Bible gets analyzed, synthesized, marginalyzed, and cognitized to meet curricular and grading requirements. Thus its affective side is overlooked and the possibility of epiphany-like experiences, in which a person receives a very personal insight into the reality and essential meaning of God's Word or an internal sense of His presence, are diminished.

The mind and emotions are means by which the will is moved. Only God knows the right combination for each particular person. The Word nourishes the mind and emotions so that the will might yield to the work of the Holy Spirit. Thus, in Christ-centered ministry the helper encourages a fellow believer to seek God through His Word and Spirit with expectancy.

Drawing Close to God through Problems

Problems of living can be seen as indicators and motivators for needed change, but even more as reasons to draw close to God, to know Him better, and to know His love which passes understanding, so that each believer might be filled with Him (Eph. 3:19). Everything in life can be used to draw or drive believers closer to God and to work His will in their lives. This is not a side issue in Scripture, second to the problems at hand. **Salvation and sanctification, or spiritual growth, are primary in perfecting the saints for loving and serving God for eternity.** As a person's life becomes more and more occupied and preoccupied with Jesus, the more spiritual growth will occur and the fruit of the Spirit will be evident. Then, instead of needing ministry, the person can be used by God to minister to others.

On the other hand, problems can also serve as temptations to sin against God and others by blaming them for misfortunes, by justifying self, and by seeking solutions that cater to the self. That is why believers are to pray for one another and

NOT succumb to offering worldly solutions. The one who ministers must continue to be faithful to the Lord and His Word so that he can say with Paul:

> Now thanks be unto God, which always causeth us to triumph in Christ, and maketh manifest the savour of his knowledge by us in every place. For we are unto God a sweet savour of Christ, in them that are saved, and in them that perish: To the one we are the savour of death unto death; and to the other the savour of life unto life. And who is sufficient for these things? For we are not as many, which corrupt the word of God: but as of sincerity, but as of God, in the sight of God speak we in Christ (2 Cor. 2:14-17).

Job and His Friends

Rather than talking about the person and his problems, true biblical ministry should be talking about God and His glorious revelation about Himself and about what He has done for all believers. Remember Job? He had his counselors who tried in vain to help him. They tried to solve his problems through reason and ended up castigating Job. While they spoke of God, they were focused on Job and his problems, until God came on the scene. When God revealed Himself to Job, who was identified in the beginning as "perfect and upright, and one that feared God, and eschewed evil" (Job 1:1), Job saw his own sinfulness, abhorred himself, and repented "in dust and ashes." He was transformed. Rather than talking about problems, the emphasis of Christ-centered ministry is to be on God and His provisions for life and godliness.

Problems can serve as trials to test the mettle of the believer and to expose that which needs to be realized, confessed, and forsaken. Some counselors too often sound like Job's first three counselors, who talked about Job and his problems and tried to expose what they thought Job needed to realize, even to the point of analyzing his motives and inner life. They pointed the finger at him, generally letting him know that his problems were the result of his own sinfulness. Job responded in a very human way, by justifying himself. At first Job cried out for an audience with God in order to set his case of suffering before Him; but after being buffeted by the accusatory analyses of his "friends," he began to justify himself and blame God for allowing bad things to happen to such a man as himself.

This is what happens in problem-centered counseling. The person and his problems are addressed, but the blame gets shifted elsewhere. Much biblical counseling continues in the same vein—talking about the person and his problems and pointing out what's wrong, such as the person's thinking, the idols of the heart, the attitude, the behavior, etc. Some biblical counseling attempts to discourage blame-shifting, to place the responsibility with the person, and to correct whatever thinking or behavior needs change. However, the human tendency is still to justify and excuse self within the heart, if not verbally. Thus, the help will not be much more than cosmetic if the main attention is still on the person and on fixing the problems. The more the attention is shifted away from the person and his problems back to God and His Word, the greater the opportunity for the person to see his own sinfulness and to repent— and for there to be deep and lasting change.

After days of listening to Job's three friends analyzing and accusing Job and of Job complaining and trying to defend himself, Elihu had heard enough. Although he was younger than the others, he dared to speak. However, Elihu took a different tack. He started by describing their unfruitful arguments and then presented truth about God and about man—the greatness of God and the spiritual depravity of man—that no one is righteous before God and that all need a ransom.

Elihu did not speak from his own experience or his own expertise; he spoke as the Spirit moved him and set forth God in His greatness and goodness. True ministry, leading to spiritual change and growth, must come from the Holy Spirit. True ministry proceeds from God Himself, whether through another believer or directly from the written Word of God. Peter declared, "If any man speak, let him speak as the oracles of God." This is what Elihu did. Although Elihu spoke truth, he could not bring Job to the point of recognizing his sin, confessing, or repenting. It was God Himself who opened Job's eyes and revealed Job to himself. **Only God can reveal the heart and change the man.**

One could liken Job's first three friends to those counselors who try to integrate the wisdom of men (psychology) with the Bible. Their wisdom was from the world and the flesh rather than from God. They relied on their own ideas, reason, experience, and theories. They analyzed, advised, diagnosed, prescribed, and judged Job. While they spoke of God, their words were such that God said to them, "Ye have not spoken of me the thing which is right, like my servant Job" (Job 42:8).

Elihu did confront Job with truth. However, he was not able to bring Job to the place he needed to be. When Elihu shifted the attention from Job to God, he was indeed moving in the right direction. Christ-centered ministry aims at bringing a person to God Himself. God challenged Job and changed him. God caused Job to see himself and repent. He then gave Job the privilege of praying for the first three counselors to receive forgiveness for their folly. Notice that Elihu was not mentioned once after God appeared to Job.

When the Lord reveals Himself through His Word and Spirit, He becomes very personal and very real. There is a special emotional and/or cognitive awareness of Christ, which leads to a response of love, worship, and submission. Job said, "I have heard of thee with the hearing of the ear: but now mine eye seeth thee. Wherefore I abhor myself, and repent in dust and ashes" (Job 42:5,6). For Job, the realization of God led to repentance. For others, the realization of God ministered to the heart may lead to peace, courage, hope, or confidence in Him. All should lead to greater love, worship, and desire to please Him.

As the Word of God is spoken or read and discussed, the Holy Spirit is the one who can pinpoint the specifics and the source within the heart for whatever behavior may appear obvious to someone else. Sins such as self-righteousness, pride, envy, bitterness, covetousness, and self-centeredness are more clearly identified by the Holy Spirit than by a fellow believer, who is limited to making guesses based on whatever behavior he has heard about or observed. When sins are thus revealed by the Holy Spirit to the inner man and as truth and grace are ministered through the Word, the hearer is less likely to defend himself before other humans, because what is happening is internal. The Holy Spirit does the work of pricking the conscience and making the application to the heart.

While there are times when a believer will confront another believer regarding known, external sin, there is no biblical justification for accusations regarding motivation or the heart. The person himself must discover the sins of the heart and attitude through the light of God's Word and applied personally by the Holy Spirit. Doctrinal truth ministered in grace through sermons, teachings, and other communications between believers and received by faith can bring forth the proper identification of sin, repentance, and change. When a person sees himself in the light of God's truth and responds in faith, defensiveness is gone and God reveals Himself as the one who has provided all things for the person's good, even as He did with Job.

Problems should bring believers to Christ instead of to the counselor's office. But too many people are in too much of a hurry to wait on the Lord. We live in a culture that demands fast relief, but Christians are called to be "in the world, but not of the world" (John 17:14-16). The psychological world says that people need such things as self-esteem, security, and significance. The Bible shows that they need to be conformed to the image of Christ. We saw how Job needed an accurate vision of God and himself and to repent in dust and ashes. The Lord allowed very severe problems into Job's life for the purpose of bringing Job to a place in which his own righteousness was not enough. God used problems of living, including loss of lives and physical disease, to further refine this "perfect and upright" man who "feared God, and eschewed evil" (Job 1:1). Even for believers who have walked with the Lord for many years, there may be seasons of problems so that God can do a deep inner work; after all, He is preparing a blemish-free bride (Eph. 5:27).

Biblical Doctrines Used

What biblical counselors often attempt to do is use verses that speak directly to the problems at hand and/or to what they think needs to be changed. In doing this they remain problem-centered, even though they are using the Bible. **The way to minister without focusing on the person and his problems would be to bring forth Scriptures that reveal God Himself.** In Christ-centered ministry, a fellow believer can bring forth essential doctrines of God and man: the greatness of God, the love of God, the great provisions of God, the new life in Christ in con-

trast to the depravity of the flesh, the conflict
between the flesh and the Spirit, the ongoing work
of Christ as our intercessor, the work of the Holy
Spirit in the life of each believer, the importance
of feeding on the Word of God, and the centrality
of prayer, worship, fellowship, and thanksgiving.

As great doctrines such as these are brought
forth in Christ-centered ministry, the Lord will do
the necessary work in the individual who responds
by grace through faith. God is the Potter. He knows
how to use circumstances, problems, and other
people to mold His children into the image of
Christ. All of these doctrines are usually taught
in every Bible-believing church. Therefore, every
believer should be familiar enough with them to
be able to minister truth and grace to one another.

The emphasis needs to be the plan of the
Potter, from the initial moment of receiving new
life in Christ, through the process of spiritual
growth in walking in the Spirit, until that day
when the believer reaches glory and sees Jesus
face to face (1 John 3:2). When believers come
together, whether or not they are experiencing
problems of living, they are to be reminding one
another of what Christ has done in saving them
and giving them new life, what He is presently
doing in working that new life in them through
the Word and the Spirit, and what He will do when
He comes again. All of this has been provided
because of God's love. It is believed and lived by
faith, and believers share the hope of His return.

Thus, the emphasis is on sharing the Word of
God, praying, and being available for helping with
whatever is needed for spiritual growth. All be-

lievers are on this path together and, while some may have more experience in walking with God and serving Him, all are equal at the foot of the cross. All are dependent upon the Lord for every breath they take and every blessing of life. God is the creator, sustainer, and ruler of the universe; He is also dwelling inside each believer, enabling each one to know and obey His law of love.

Those who seek counseling or personal ministry may have reached a place in life in which they are being challenged to trust God more and to discover that in Christ they themselves have spiritual resources to deal with personal, inter-personal, or situational problems. During difficult times members of the Body of Christ can assist one another through the various means given in Scripture. The Lord desires that the Body of Christ work together, serve together, worship together, learn together, and pray together. He does not want us isolated from one another. He wants us to be fellowshipping with one another, loving one another, encouraging one another, worshipping together, and hearing the Word of God together on a regular basis.

> Let us hold fast the profession of our faith without wavering; (for he is faithful that promised;) And let us consider one another to provoke unto love and to good works: Not forsaking the assembling of ourselves together, as the manner of some is; but exhorting one another: and so much the more, as ye see the day approaching (Heb. 10:23-25).

Problems of living can serve as catalysts for members of the Body of Christ to do just that.

Spiritual Growth through Problems of Living

Problems of living are some of the best means of bringing believers to the end of themselves wherein they recognize the flesh for what it really is and are willing to put it off and to put on the "new man, which after God is created in righteousness and true holiness" (Eph. 4:22-24). Problems provide opportunities for spiritual growth.

Both Jesus and the writers of the Epistles viewed problems as circumstances to be expected. Believers were not to expect a less problem-free life than their Lord's. They also considered difficulties to have a purpose:

> That the trial of your faith, being much more precious than of gold that perisheth, though it be tried with fire, might be found unto praise and honour and glory at the appearing of Jesus Christ (1 Peter 1:7).

Paul even went so far as to rejoice in his suffering both for the sake of Christ and for the opportunity to know Christ in His suffering (Phil. 3:10). And James declared:

> My brethren, count it all joy when ye fall into divers temptations. Knowing this, that

the trying of your faith worketh patience (James 1:2,3).

A believer who is walking in the Spirit will want to glorify God in the midst of problems and can be confident that God will show the way through them. Thus more attention needs to be given to the Lord than to the problems. That does not mean that practical steps would not be taken to change circumstances or behavior, but they would be taken according to the will of God as revealed in His Word and applied by the Holy Spirit in the individual.

In investigating why people change, researchers have determined that the number one reason why people change is personal motivation. Just as Paul tells us to "provoke" one another "to love and good works," even so we are to encourage each other to think about God and all that He has provided for both spiritual and physical life. As each one responds in faith, hope, and love, there will be change and growth. The Holy Spirit will both motivate and enable the kind of change that each believer should be making daily—putting off the old ways of the flesh, being "renewed in the spirit of the mind," and putting "on the new man, which after God is created in righteousness and true holiness" (Eph. 4:22-24).

If we pursue spiritual growth with one another, we should not major on problems, but rather on Christ's provisions. In Christ there is hope, wisdom, truth, and love. These should motivate a person to seek Him first and to seek His will concerning all circumstances. The one who comes alongside to minister does not need to be involved in directing the other as to what to do or how to do it. His main function is to speak biblical truth and point the person to the Lord. Only the Lord knows what He is working on next in each one of His children. He can bring conviction to the heart, renew the mind, and enable change.

Some people may want to help an individual change those things that are most obvious, such as certain behaviors. However, it may be that the Lord will work through a different order. For instance, a particular person may first need a greater understanding of God's love and a greater desire to love and please Him. In other words, the Lord knows the right procedure and order for each person. That is why preaching the Word, teaching the Bible, praying, worshipping, and fellowshipping are so effective. The Holy Spirit can take that Word and make the application to each individual.

While we may be able to help motivate one another to seek the Lord through teaching, encouraging, admonishing, and drawing alongside to help, sanctification is accomplished through the Lord working in the individual as that individual responds in faith and obedience (Phil. 2:12,13). If sinful habits and responses are firmly ingrained through past repetition, a great deal of motivation is necessary. However, believers who are coming to know God's great love for them and also recognizing their own depravity apart from Him will desire to please Him. As they grow spiritually they will change even if particular works of the flesh are not directly addressed during Christ-centered ministry. In other words, when two or more people come together to talk, they do not need to be preoccupied with one or more specific sins, such as sinful anger or drunkenness. The Holy Spirit can take the Word of God and apply it to the next thing that needs change. While there are times when believers need to be rebuked directly, as described in 1 Corinthians 5, these are matters of discipline, not "counseling."

Ministering to One Another

As one moves away from problem-centered counseling to Christ-centered ministry, by allowing the problems of living to serve as catalysts for spiritual growth, motivation will increase and people will change, even if circumstances and other people do not change. If you have an issue or problem, the best resolution is not always by circumstances or another person changing. In fact, any fleshly resolution or cure will only strengthen the flesh, which is to be denied, and may obviate the opportunity for spiritual growth. As a matter of fact, the deeper and more difficult the problem or circumstance one is facing, the greater the opportunity for spiritual growth.

Can you see the difference between the usual process of counseling and the way the Lord works in His children through His Word, the Holy Spirit, and the Body of Christ? We all need to move away from the problem-centered counseling to which people have become accustomed. We need to shift the attention back to the goal of loving God and becoming like Christ, rather than making life more comfortable and pleasant for self. Even though biblical counselors use biblical teachings, the very process of problem-centered counseling and the very relationship of counselor (expert) and counselee (person who becomes the center of attention) can serve to hinder each person's dynamic dependence on God and faith in His full provision for all things pertaining to life and godliness (2 Peter 1:2-4).

6

Who, What Why, When, Where & How

If we throw out the psychological way and fail to dip into a compromised way, what is left? An abundance that many Christians are not fully utilizing! We have the Lord and His Word, which is the only truly and totally valid truth about mankind. We have the new life in Christ, which is complete. "For in him dwelleth all the fulness of the Godhead bodily. And ye are complete in him, which is the head of all principality and power" (Col. 2:9,10). And, we have the Holy Spirit's ongoing work of sanctification in every believer! Christians have far more spiritual resources than they use both for living their own lives and for ministering the life of Christ to others!

One of Satan's primary ways of working is to overshadow and undermine the real with a deceptively flawed facsimile. **Therefore we are calling believers back to the Lord and His Word and back to their new life in Christ,**

**totally without the aid of psychology and
totally without the use of biblical counseling manuals, seminars, conferences, workshops, degrees and certificates! And, totally
accomplished at the local church level.**

Ordinary believers have mined and can mine
these tremendous spiritual resources for their own
lives and for those around them. In fact, many
believers are already equipped to minister and
indeed are already ministering to one another in
those Bible-believing churches where the doctrines
of Scripture are faithfully preached, taught, and
used for evangelism; where believers are earnestly
responding to the Word in obedience and ongoing
application; and where believers are growing in
their love for God and one another. They may not
realize that they are equipped or that they are
already ministering to one another in ways that
are far superior to anything offered by counseling
psychology or by the biblical counseling movement.

Here is a brief summary of Who, What, Why,
When, Where, and How of ministering to one
another in the Body of Christ. Not only should
every mature believer who reads this say, "I can
do this through Christ"; some will say, "God is
already doing this through me!"

Who

Three persons are involved whenever there is
personal ministry in the Body of Christ. The
primary person is the Lord Himself! The second
person is the one in need. And, the third person,

who pales in comparison and must take a humble position, is the believer who comes alongside.

The Lord works in each believer through His Word and the Holy Spirit. He is the Potter who is forming each believer into the image of Christ. He has provided all that is necessary for life and godliness (2 Peter 1:3). He is always present and knows the end from the beginning and uses all circumstances for the ultimate good of each of His spiritual children. He both directs change and equips believers to know truth and to obey.

Those in need. Jesus invites people experiencing difficult life issues to come to Him. He said:

> Come unto me, all ye that labour and are heavy laden, and I will give you rest. Take my yoke upon you, and learn of me; for I am meek and lowly in heart: and ye shall find rest unto your souls. For my yoke is easy, and my burden is light (Matt. 11:29-30).

He calls people to be yoked together with Him, to learn from Him, and to follow His ways. He will guide and direct through the difficult places. But notice that the person is not passive, but active. There must be cooperation with what the Lord is doing. The person must be willing to follow Christ in obedience and spiritual growth, even when it involves suffering. While the Lord enables, the believers choose whether or not to obey.

Those who come alongside are small players in the drama of sanctification going on in a

fellow believer's life. However, they themselves
must be seeking the same goal in their own lives,
that is, to be conformed to the image of Christ.
They themselves must be learning how to walk
according to their new life in Christ, rather than
according to the old ways of the flesh. They must
be following Christ, denying self, trusting the Lord
and acknowledging Him throughout each day.
Those who come alongside will be leading fellow
believers in the same direction they themselves
are going. They do not have to be perfect, but they
must be growing in Christ, because one who is
walking according to the flesh and not attempting to put off the flesh along with its deceitful lusts
can hardly minister sanctification to a fellow
believer.

When ministry is one-to-one outside the
family, we advise men to minister to men, women
to women, and married couples to married couples.
Not only does this arrangement avoid sexual temptation, but it also avoids having a woman usurp
authority over a man. In addition, only a man
knows what it is to follow Christ in his manhood
and in the roles of leadership he has been given in
the family and church. Only a woman knows what
it is to follow Christ in her womanhood and in the
role requiring submission to a spouse. Scripture
has numerous examples of men ministering to
men, and Scripture calls the older women to
minister to the younger ones.

> The aged women likewise, that they be in
> behaviour as becometh holiness, not false
> accusers, not given to much wine, teachers

of good things; that they may teach the young women to be sober, to love their husbands, to love their children, to be discreet, chaste, keepers at home, good, obedient to their own husbands, that the word of God be not blasphemed (Titus 2:3-5).

Notice how the person's life teaches as well as the words. Throughout Scripture we see such examples of how a great deal of teaching and ministry in the Body of Christ is by example—by simply living the new life rather than the old. When believers serve as living epistles, there is no gender distinction. What is important here is what is being ministered: the new life or the old.

What

Paul preached Christ and Him crucified, because the Gospel is central for all of the Christian's life, not just for initial salvation (which is called justification), but for the entire subsequent walk with Christ (which is called sanctification) and on to glorification. This central theme of the Gospel begins and ends with the love of God that passes understanding as revealed in the Bible. The Gospel includes such essential teachings as the holiness of God, the depravity of the natural man, the love of God, the cross of Christ, the new life in Christ, and the ongoing work of the Holy Spirit. Whatever is ministered must be faithful to the Lord and His Word.

Believers are called to minister truth—to use God's Word, empowered by the Holy Spirit, to minister to one another. Scripture is God's truth about Himself and about mankind. God has demonstrated His love through His Word and through all that Christ did to secure our salvation and to give us new life. Through His Word, God has also revealed the inner man of all people born upon this earth. He has revealed their heart, their spiritual condition, and the nature of their soul. Moreover He has provided the only means of real change—from spiritual death to new life. He has provided the only means of nourishing that new life: through His Word, His Spirit, and His Body. The new life must have spiritual food and cannot be nourished through the wisdom or ways of the world. Therefore the Word of God is to be ministered by the indwelling Holy Spirit and by the life of Christ ministered to one another in the Body of Christ.

The Word of God is a vast resource. It provides all the information one needs for being saved and sanctified, for knowing God's love, for loving God and one another, for living the new life in Christ, for denying self, and for spiritual warfare. The Word of God is powerful and the doctrines of Scripture are dynamic. **There's more power, wisdom, healing and help in any truth from Scripture than from all the psychological theories and therapies** conceived by those who devised or utilize the nearly 500 different systems of psychotherapy.

Why

The "why" for all ministry is for God to be glorified, people to be saved and sanctified, and the Body of Christ to be edified until He comes again. If an unbeliever seeks ministry, the primary ministry should be to present the Gospel as clearly as possible. The Gospel should be the focus until a person is saved or decides to discontinue the ministering relationship. Once a person is born again he is a new person. "Therefore if any man be in Christ, he is a new creature: old things are passed away; behold, all things are become new" (2 Cor 5:17). From that point on the purpose of ministry is to guide and encourage the believers to walk according to their new life in Christ rather than according to the old ways of the flesh.

Every believer has numerous opportunities to grow spiritually. God uses all circumstances to bring this about. Therefore the **primary purpose for ministry must be spiritual growth rather than problem solving**. The Apostle Paul's goal was to present every believer perfect in Christ and that is the goal of Christ-centered, biblical ministry as well.

Most people seek counseling to solve their problems or to cause another person to change, but true biblical ministry is for the purpose of sanctification and spiritual growth. However, problems can serve as broken ground for the Lord, and the person who comes alongside has the opportunity to plant seed and nurture growth. Consider the

following reasons for ministry that encourages
spiritual growth:

1. When we give attention to the Lord and His
   Word we are enabled to grow spiritually and
   to better deal with problems of living. This
   is all through relationship with Christ as
   He described with the analogy of the vine
   and the branches in John 15:1-11.

2. God has a plan and purpose for every one
   of His children. He is the Potter and uses
   all things in a believer's life to complete the
   work of conforming each one to the image
   of Christ. (Romans 8:28-29).

3. The problems themselves can be used as
   catalysts for spiritual growth. See, for example, James 1:2-4 and 1 Peter 5:10.

4. Problems can serve to bring us to the end
   of ourselves (flesh) and make us more
   dependent on Christ to guide us and lead
   us as we take His yoke upon us (Matt. 11:28-
   30).

5. Problems can serve to put a person in a
   position to comprehend God more fully, to
   recognize the flesh for what it is, to abhor
   it, to deny self, and to seek God's will and
   wisdom (Job 42).

6. As a person draws close to God through
   trials, he will grow spiritually (1 Peter 1:6-
   8). We see examples throughout Scripture
   of where people drew close to God in afflic-
   tion and became fruitful for Him (King
   David, the apostle Paul, and those in the

early church). See 2 Cor. 4:7-11 and 2 Cor. 12:6-10 for example.

7. Spiritual growth enables people to walk pleasing to God and to be equipped for the trials of life. This principle is woven throughout Scripture. See, for example, Ephesians 4.

8. Problems of living signal that spiritual warfare is taking place. The battle involves the world, the flesh, and the devil. As a believer recognizes and acts on the truths of 2 Cor. 10:3-6; Galatians 5:16,17; Ephesians 6:10-18; and 1 Peter 5:8-10, he will grow spiritually and learn how to deal with problems of living according to what the Lord has provided.

9. As people recognize all that Christ is in them, they will gain courage for the present and hope for the future. As they learn to walk according to their life in Him, their lives will be transformed as described in Colossians 3.

10. Growing spiritually brings forth the fruit of the Spirit: "But the fruit of the Spirit is love, joy, peace, longsuffering, gentleness, goodness, faith, meekness, temperance: against such there is no law" (Gal. 5:22-23).

The goal of spiritual growth is far greater than present problem solving. The benefits so outweigh any other course of action that every believer should jump at the chance to use everything possible for spiritual growth, to be conformed to the image of Christ, and to live to the glory of God.

When

The best time for spiritual growth is when a person is most receptive to the Lord, and this is often when the life is being torn up by problems. When difficult circumstances jolt a person out of everyday routine and even complacency, that person may be ready to face the depravity of the flesh, turn to the cross, and be ready to change. That is why Jesus called those who recognized their spiritual needs "blessed" (Matt. 5:3-6). They are ready and open for change and spiritual growth. This is when they may well benefit from a fellow believer to come along and encourage such growth. If they are sent off to psychological or psychologically tainted counseling, a wonderful spiritual opportunity is wasted and maturity postponed.

Just as preaching is to be in season and out of season, so should believers be ready to mutually care for one another and encourage one another even when it is not convenient. **There is a time for planting, when the ground is torn up, and there is a time for watering after the seed has been sown.** As believers we are all to be ready to give an answer for the hope that is in us (1 Peter 3:15). We also need to be ready to share that hope with one another during times of trouble and discouragement. Therefore, personal ministry can occur any time, every time there is a need and an opportunity for spiritual growth, and all the time as our lives touch one another in the Body of Christ.

Where

Ministry should be ongoing in the home, the church, and beyond. Because mutual care in the Body of Christ is not a counseling profession, there is no need for an office with walls covered by degrees and certificates. Believers can meet anywhere that works for them—in their homes, in the church building, at a park, or at a restaurant. They could even decide to go for a walk together. Some conversations do require more privacy than others do, but anyone can figure that out. Christians can be creative regarding a place to meet. But, the where should be at the local level without outside assistance from the biblical counseling movement.

How

The conversation of caring for one another in the Body of Christ is not a professional interchange between a so-called expert and a client or between a counselor and counselee. It is between two or more believers who are learning to walk in the Spirit and encouraging one another to do so. Since the Holy Spirit is ministering the truth of God's Word to all involved in the conversation, Christ-centered ministry cannot be done according to the flesh or human ingenuity. The how of Christ-centered ministry is believers seeking the Lord together.

> But speaking the truth in love, may grow up into him in all things, which is the head, even Christ: From whom the whole body

> fitly joined together and compacted by that
> which every joint supplieth, according to the
> effectual working in the measure of every
> part, maketh increase of the body unto the
> edifying of itself in love (Eph. 4:15,16).

Both the helper and the seeker are growing
together.

Much of what the helper will do during
ministry is reminding the seeker of whatever
truths of Scripture are needed during the conversation.

> Wherefore I will not be negligent to put you
> always in remembrance of these things,
> though ye know them, and be established
> in the present truth (2 Peter 1:12).

We encourage believers to remember what
they already know, because problems of living may
have so absorbed their attention and clouded their
vision that they need to be reminded of the
relevance of Scripture to their circumstances and
of the presence of God working in their lives. Other
Christians may need to be taught. There are individuals in each congregation who are unsaved or
who are naïve or ignorant of biblical doctrines
having to do with living the Christian life. In either
case, the reminding and teaching must be done in
humility and lowliness, not from a position of
superiority.

While God is the central person in any biblical ministry, we emphasize the responsibility of
the seeker to trust God and to obey what He has

revealed. God will guide and enable, but the person must do. Ministering helpers can come alongside according to Galatians 6, but in the final analysis, it is the seeker's own actions that count. Notice the humility of ministry and the burden of responsibility on the one who receives ministry.

> Brethren, if a man be overtaken in a fault, ye which are spiritual, restore such an one in the spirit of meekness; considering thyself, lest thou also be tempted. Bear ye one another's burdens, and so fulfil the law of Christ. For if a man think himself to be something, when he is nothing, he deceiveth himself. But let every man prove his own work, and then shall he have rejoicing in himself alone, and not in another. **For every man shall bear his own burden** (Gal. 6:1-5).

We emphasize personal responsibility for change and growth according to all of God's provisions for walking according to the Spirit. For too long people have been taught to see themselves as helpless victims rather than responsible persons. For too long the professional counseling industry has been in the business of manufacturing victims. Psychotherapists help people find the source of their problems in their parents and in their circumstances. Rather than manufacturing victims, Christ-centered ministry should bring salvation to the sinner and sanctification of the saint, thus encouraging that person to walk in the fullness of what God has provided in Christ.

As we demonstrated earlier, the more motivated the individual, the more likely that change
will occur. Thus, the helper will encourage motivation through the application of mercy and truth,
grace and justice, nurture and admonition. There
are no formulas for how much of each, and it's
usually not one or the other of these applications,
but a subtle combination, which is different for
each person at each encounter. Sound impossible?
Yes, without the Lord, one would have to try to
follow a manual or use the guessing procedure
discussed earlier. But, remember. This is the Lord's
work. The work of the Holy Spirit is essential in
Christ-centered ministry.

Only the Lord knows how much of mercy and
truth to apply. Sometimes a suffering soul needs
a gentle word emphasizing the mercy, grace, and
nurture of the Lord, His love and caring. At other
times a fellow believer would be motivated better
by a direct word of truth, emphasizing God's justice
and serving as an admonition. At each moment,
the ministering helper must listen with both the
physical ear and the inner ear. The Lord is faithful to lead as He is acknowledged in the heart every
moment throughout any time of ministry.

By reading through the epistles of the New
Testament, one will find numerous admonitions
of how believers are to treat one another and these
show ways in which members of the Body of Christ
can minister to one another. Jesus ministered
differently to each person, because He knew each
one's need. He still does, and those who minister
to one another need to follow Him in being sensi-
tive to what is needful for each person. Paul gave

a brief example of ministering differently to each individual: "Now we exhort you, brethren, warn them that are unruly, comfort the feebleminded, support the weak, be patient toward all men" (1Thes. 5:14). Remember that personal ministry is the Lord's creative work through one believer ministering to another.

First and foremost, we are to love fellow believers. Jesus said we are to love one another as He has loved us. That means to love one another sacrificially (John 15:12,13), without regard for a person's wealth or station in life (Romans 12:16; James 2:1-24). Paul reminds believers to "be kindly affectioned one to another with brotherly love; in honour preferring one another" (Rom. 12:10). That means putting the other person first. Love is something freely given, without charge.

Just plain fellowship among Christians is a blessing. Here is where love can be given and received. Fellowship nurtures mutual care and encouragement. Talking about the Lord and how He is working in our own lives can do more to strengthen us in the Lord than endless counseling sessions. Hebrews 10:24-25 instructs us:

> And let us consider one another to provoke unto love and to good works: Not forsaking the assembling of ourselves together, as the manner of some is; but exhorting one another: and so much the more, as ye see the day approaching.

This encouragement and exhortation should be an ongoing interaction among believers. Our fellow-

ship is first of all with our Father and our Lord
Jesus Christ (1 John 1:3). Next, our fellowship is
with other believers: "But if we walk in the light,
as he is in the light, we have fellowship one with
another, and the blood of Jesus Christ his Son
cleanseth us from all sin" (1 John 1:7). This fellowship is far deeper than casual relationships.
We are connected with one another in Christ in
that we are formed together as His Body (Eph.
2:21,22).

Our greatest desire is to encourage people to
draw closer to God—to look to Him and to love,
serve, and obey Him. While drawing people closer
to God may not change their circumstances, it will
accomplish far more on the inside. As people are
encouraged to draw close to God, they will find
His perspective as well as His provision and His
will as well as His willingness to help. Every
believer can be a source of encouragement.

Expressing the Life of Christ

Christ-centered ministry is reflecting and
expressing the Life of Christ. How one does that
is truly a mystery. It is the mystery of "Christ in
you, the hope of glory" (Col. 1:27). It is a spiritual
activity of Jesus Christ Himself through the Holy
Spirit and through members of His Body. Therefore, the how of ministry is not a methodology but
Jesus working through believers as they come
together. Christ must be preeminent in all the
thinking, speaking, and doing among members of
His Body. If He is at the center, true ministry
happens. Life comes forth and people are blessed!

7

Christ-Centered Ministry versus Problem-Centered Counseling

Christ-centered ministry encourages spiritual growth and depends on the Lord to do the work in each individual through His Word and Spirit. Therefore, one can confidently assure believers that this ministry is more effective, long-lasting, and spiritually rewarding than problem-centered counseling for those who are willing to go this way. For those who follow this Christ-centered ministry there will be spiritual growth, even if certain problems at hand are not resolved.

Because Christ-centered ministry utilizes all that should already be available in every Bible-believing church where Christians are growing in the Lord, it avoids what we call the "onerous ones" that typify problem-centered counseling. We briefly touched on these onerous ones earlier. However, we will expand on them here to clarify some

major differences between Christ-centered
ministry and problem-centered counseling for the
purpose of encouraging believers to take courage
in exercising their gifts, talents, and responsibili-
ties for ministering to one another without fear or
intimidation from the counseling world.

One to One

Problem-centered counseling is typically a
one-to-one relationship. Sometimes couples and
families are involved, but the relationship is generally artificial and restrictive. The counseling
relationship itself usually does not extend outside
the counseling room. The relationship lasts as long
as counseling is being provided and normally does
not extend to other involvement, even in most
biblical counseling centers. Problem-centered
counselors commonly do not involve themselves
with counselees outside the counseling room. That
is why both psychological and biblical counselors
sometimes use intake forms requesting a great
deal of personal information. Because this relationship is generally isolated, the counselor and
counselee can be selective as to what they want to
reveal about themselves. In fact, as we mentioned
earlier, research shows that counselees often lie
to their counselors and protect themselves by
concealing important information.

The great advantage of Christ-centered ministry is that it is not limited to an artificial one-to-
one relationship where one has the problem and
the other supposedly has the solution. In the Body
of Christ all are growing together. There are many

opportunities to know one another and to inter-
act in genuine relationships. When a believer is
experiencing problems, more than one person may
be involved in ministering to that individual. One
may be teaching. One may be reminding. Another
may simply be extending support and fellowship.
Another may be helping in practical ways. Another
may be exhorting. Another may be admonishing.
And, in a few cases, some may be exercising the
responsibility of disciplining a fellow believer for
the sake of restoration. But, all can be praying
and encouraging the individual in the direction of
the Lord. And, through all this, all are growing
together and the relationships may deepen with
one another as well as with the Lord.

One Day a Week

Problem-centered counseling is generally one-
to-one, one-day-a-week, but rarely outside the
office. Someone pointed out the paradox of the
counseling relationship by saying that while the
relationship is extremely intimate at times, the
counselor has no interest in seeing the counselee
outside the office. Many problem-centered counselors, including biblical counselors, avoid other
contacts with their counselees, who cannot see the
counselor outside the prescribed one-day-a-week,
unless additional appointments are made.

In Christ-centered ministry the possibilities
of seeing one another and communicating by
phone are only limited by the number of individuals available. As mentioned earlier, Christians can
choose when and how often to meet together for

personal ministry. In the body of Christ this can be done freely without the one-day-a-week time constraints of problem-centered counseling

One Hour

In addition to the one-to-one and one-day-a-week errors in most problem-centered counseling, there is generally the fifty-minute hour limitation. Why a fifty-minute hour or similar restriction? The time restriction is a device to meet the needs of problem-centered counselors to regulate the flow of counselees for convenience and sometimes for income. This relationship governed by the clock benefits the counselor, not the counselee. And, if the counselee is late, the already reduced hour is further reduced; if the counselee is desperate and needs more time, it is already taken by other counselees.

Christ-centered ministry is governed by love rather than the clock. Giving time to a fellow believer is a way of saying, "I care about you." And because the ministry is shared among believers, it supersedes what is available or affordable in problem-centered counseling. A local church is not bound by the one-to-one, one-day-a-week, one-hour relationships of problem-centered counseling.

One Week after Another

One-to-one, one-day-a-week and one-hour shortcomings of problem-centered counseling are amplified by one-week-after-another. As mentioned earlier, Mesmer and Freud began what resulted in today's problem-centered counseling. Freud's system of psychoanalysis actually involved three to five sessions per week and lasted over a period of years. Thus he set the pattern for long-term therapy. Today many problem-centered counselors continue to retain counselees over numerous weeks, months, and even years in spite of research that shows no advantage of long-term counseling. Long-term counseling relationships also deteriorate into dependency relationships. People in problem-centered counseling often become dependent on their counselors rather than on the Lord.

In contrast, Christ-centered ministry emphasizes dependency on the Lord Himself, and in a church where the ministries are functioning and the gifts are operating, the mutual care and encouragement of fellow believers are there to assist all believers in their ongoing walk with the Lord. Rather than a long-term artificial counseling relationship there is a relationship of mutual care in which believers are available to encourage one another as they are growing together in Christ.

One Fixed Price
The one-to-one, one-day-a-week, one-hour, one-week-after-another errors of problem-centered counseling lead to one fixed price that is charged (or a donation that is expected). Some biblical counselors charge fees or request donations for their services for some of the same reasons as psychological counselors. The establishing, billing and collecting of fees (or encouraging of donations) are a significant aspect of most problem-centered counseling. Because of salaries to be paid, the one

fixed price (or donation) becomes a necessity that limits the relationship. If one cannot pay his bill (or contribute) the relationship is usually over. The money paid (or donated) must match the mark in the appointment book and the hand on the clock. After all, a problem-centered counselor who charges a fee must fill enough appointments to make a desirable income.

There is no example in Scripture for charging a fee (or asking for a donation) for ministering the Word of God by the grace of God to a brother or sister in Christ. Someone might protest that a minister is paid a salary. But that is a false analogy. The true analogy would be charging someone a fee to attend church. Christ-centered ministry is freely given just as Jesus gave freely of His life and love. He said, "Love one another, as I have loved you"(John 15:12). When Jesus sent His disciples to minister, he said to them, "Freely ye have received, freely give" (Matt. 10:8). Believers are to reach out to one another in love, friendship, and mutual care as they are all growing together as members of one body.

One Right after Another

One right after another fits right into the one-to-one, one-day-a-week, one-hour, one-week-after-another, and one-fixed-price onerosities. In problem-centered counseling there is usually a progression of one person right after another. Counselees know others have preceded them and others will follow. No one has set a limit on how many counselees per day one counselor can effectively manage. Counseling eight hours a day, five days a week, with large numbers of people always has and always will lead to superficial relationships lacking genuine compassion, even in the biblical counseling office. There is no biblical example for one-right-after-another, problem-centered counseling. No, not even the example of Moses, since he was judging disputes between people, rather than getting into the pattern of problem-centered counseling as practiced today.

In Christ-centered ministry, the personal ministry load can be spread among many believers. There is no need for one-right-after-another or the other onerous ones. There is often a temptation for the pastor or a paid staff member to carry the load of personal ministry. When this happens, one right after another can weaken the overall ministry, overburden the pastoral staff, and be affected by the onerous ones. Believers need to learn to minister to one another and to receive ministry from each other rather than depending on the pastor or a staff counselor for such help.

One Up/One Down

The one-to-one, one-day-a-week, one-hour, one-week-after-another, one-fixed-price, one-right-after-another are eclipsed in problem-centered counseling by the tragic onerosity of the one-up/one-down relationship, with the counselor considered as the expert with the gnosis to perform the cure. This artificial hierarchy of the expert over the needy one is unbiblical and not supported by the research, as we have demonstrated elsewhere.

Rather than an expert being responsible to fix the problem, Christ-centered ministry draws both the seeker and the helper to the Lord for wisdom and transformation. When the Lord calls one believer to minister to another believer, both are seeking the Lord in meekness and humility. Believers may be especially gifted to minister to one another in the faith, but all (even those in leadership) stand on an equal plain at the foot of the cross. Indeed, it is the Lord who truly accomplishes the restoration and sanctification of the believer.

Our Goal

Our goal is to remind believers of their call and empowerment to serve in the Body of Christ. Obviously not all the necessary information regarding Christ-centered ministry is in this short book, but the Lord will bring forth what is missing through the Holy Spirit, the Word of God, and the Body of Christ as you seek to serve Him. He will give you opportunities to grow spiritually and serve according to His will, through His Word, and by grace through faith.

We seek to encourage ministry and to discourage the use of problem-centered counseling. We seek to encourage dependence on the Lord and His Word to minister to one another in the Body of Christ, without intimidation by or dependence on biblical counseling manuals, workshops, seminars, degrees, or certificates. We hope to see ministry shared among believers in their local fellowships with their focus on Jesus Christ and the Word of God. The Lord will enable them to serve as they are constant in prayer, diligent in Bible study, and marked with the humility of a servant's heart and as they are ready to serve without having to be in a superior position or to have a title of superiority. Ministry among believers should be constant and ongoing, which will result in souls beset with problems seeking the Lord through His Spirit, Word, and Body rather than turning to counselors trained in psychological or biblical counseling. We hope this book will encourage you to participate in what God is doing and will do in the lives of His children. What a privilege to be included in the mighty, miraculous work of God in one another's lives. All believers have opportunities to minister to fellow believers to encourage them along the way.

What a blessing it would be if there were an end to problem-centered counseling and a restoration of Christ-centered ministry in the Body of Christ. Restoring Christ-centered ministry should lead to the end of both the psychological and biblical counseling movements in the church. **We urge those who call themselves biblical counselors to move away from problem-centeredness and to abandon and condemn the unbiblical practices of: charging fees, operating separated from the church centers, using psychological integration, belonging to psychological or integrationist organizations, using the terms *counselor*, *counselee*, and *counseling*, and practicing one or more of the other onerous ones.**

As we have said, "The biblical counseling movement must die." It must die to the unbiblical practices, to which it has been shackled and been reluctant to condemn. It must remove itself so that Christians in local congregations can minister as they should, without outside intimidation or interference. Pastors, elders, and church leaders must bear the responsibility for such a move or admit they have failed at what they have been biblically called to do. Christians in their local congregations are also responsible to encourage and be open to such a move and to be involved in such ministry as a helper and/or seeker. We hope and pray that our small voice, along with others who already truly minister biblically, will be heard and heeded.

If you are one who is experiencing problems of living and looking for assistance, find someone in your local church who can minister to you. Find someone who is mature in the faith and is walking with God the way you desire to walk. Ask that person to come alongside, minister the Life of Christ, speak forth the truth of God, encourage you in your walk with the Lord, and earnestly pray.

If you are a Christian, know essential biblical doctrines, are walking according to your new life in Christ and growing in the Lord, you already have what it takes to minister the Life of Christ to a fellow believer. You have a living God, the source of all life and healing. You have His living, enduring, abiding Word (1 Peter 1:23-25), which ministers truth to the mind, direction and encouragement to the will, and grace for the emotions. Christ-centered ministry is not a position of expertise (one-up-man-ship) but one of side-by-side seeking the Lord. It does not lead believers into the downward spiral of problems, but rather upward to the Life of Christ and the Word of God through the work of the Holy Spirit. Can you think of anything more worthwhile than to serve God in your own family, in the Body of Christ, and in the world? Every person in whom the Holy Spirit lives is enabled to serve and can say with Paul, "I can do all things through Christ which strengtheneth me" (Phil. 4:13)? Take courage! God will indeed work His own good pleasure in and through His children.

SOLI DEO GLORIA

Notes

Chapter 1: A Radical Proposal

1. See Martin and Deidre Bobgan. *PsychoHeresy: The Psychological Seduction of Christianity* (1987); *The End of "Christian Psychology"* (1997); and *Against "Biblical Counseling": For the Bible* (1994). Santa Barbara, CA: EastGate Publishers; articles from *PsychoHeresy Awareness Letter* now posted on <www.psychoheresy-aware.org>.

Chapter 2: Psychotherapy (Talk Therapy)

1. Ellen Herman. *The Romance of American Psychology: Political Culture in the Age of Experts.* Berkeley: University of California Press, 1996, p. 1.
2. *Ibid.*, p. 3.
3. *Ibid.*, p. 5.
4. *Ibid.*, p. 311.
5. *Ibid.*, p. 315.
6. APA Commission on Psychotherapies. *Psychotherapy Research: Methodological and Efficacy Issues.* Washington, DC: American Psychiatric Association, 1982.
7. Mary Sykes Wylie interviewing Martin Seligman. "Why Is This Man Smiling?" *Psychotherapy Networker*, Vol. 27, No. 1, p. 51.
8. Leslie Prioleau, Martha Murdock, and Nathan Brody. "An Analysis of Psychotherapy Versus Placebo Studies," *The Behavioral and Brain Sciences*, June 1983, p. 284.
9. Arthur Shapiro interview by Martin Gross. *The Psychological Society.* New York: Random House, 1978, p. 230.
10. Arthur Shapiro, "Opening Comments" in *Psychotherapy Research*, Janet B. W. Williams and Robert L. Spitzer, eds. New York: The Guilford Press, 1984, p. 106.
11. *Ibid.*, p. 107.
12. H. J. Eysenck, "The Outcome Problem in Psychotherapy: What Have We Learned?" *Behavioural Research and Therapy*, Vol. 32, No. 5, 1994, p.490.
13. Michael J. Lambert and Allen E. Bergin. "The Effectiveness of Psychotherapy" in *Handbook of Psychotherapy and Behavior Change*, Fourth Edition, Allen E. Bergin and Sol L. Garfield, eds. New York: John Wiley & Sons, Inc., 1994, p. 161.
14. Joseph Wortis. "General Discussion" in *Psychotherapy Research*, Janet B. W Williams and Robert L. Spitzes, eds. New York: The Guilford Press, 1984, p. 394.

15. *Harvard Mental Health Letter*, Vol. 16, No. 11, p. 21.
16. *Journal of Studies on Alcohol*, Vol. 58, pp. 7-29.
17. D. A. Shapiro quoted in *Placebo: Theory, Research, and Mechanisms*, Leonard White, Bernard Tursky and Gary E. Schwartz, eds. New York: The Guilford Press, 1985, p. 204.
18. Robyn Dawes, *House of Cards: Psychology and Psychotherapy Built on Myth*. New York: The Free Press/ Macmillan, Inc., 1994, p. 62.
19. *Ibid.*, p. 15.
20. *Ibid* .,p. 58.
21. Carol Tavris. "Psychological Warfare between Therapists and Scientists," *Chronicle of High Education*, February 28, 2003.
22. See Martin and Deidre Bobgan. *Against "Biblical Counseling": For the Bible* (1994) and *Competent to Minister: The Biblical Care of Souls* (1996). Santa Barbara. CA: EastGate Publishers.
23. Sigmund Koch. "Psychology Cannot Be a Coherent Science," *Psychology Today*. September 1969, p. 66.
24. Karl Popper. "Scientific Theory and Falsifiability" in *Perspectives in Philosophy*, Robert N. Beck, ed. New York: Holt, Rinehart, Winston, 1975, p. 343.
25. Linda Riebel. "Theory as Self-Portrait and the Ideal of Objectivity," *Journal of Humanistic Psychology*, Spring 1982, pp. 91-92.

Chapter 3: The Biblical Counseling Movement

1. Ellen Herman. *The Romance of American Psychology: Political Culture in the Age of Experts*. Berkeley: University of California Press, 1996.
2. Elizabeth F. Loftus and Melvin J. Guyer. "Who Abused Jane Doe? The Hazards of the Single Case History," Part 1. *Skeptical Inquirer*, Vol. 26, No. 3, p. 24.
3. *Ibid.*, p. 25.
4. Paul E. Meehl. *Psychodiagnosis: Selected Papers*. Minneapolis: University of Minnesota Press, 1973.
5. Allen E. Bergin and Sol L. Garfield, "Overview, Trends, and Future Issues" in *Handbook of Psychotherapy and Behavior Change*, Fourth Edition, Allen E. Bergin and Sol L. Garfield, eds. New York: John Wiley & Sons, Inc., 1994, p. 825.
6. *Journal of Studies on Alcohol*, Vol. 58, pp. 7-29.
7. *Harvard Mental Health Letter*, Vol. 16, No. 12, pp. 1-4.
8. Bruce E. Wampold. *The Great Psychotherapy Debate*. Mahwah, NJ: Lawrence Erlbaum Publishers, p. ix.

9. Joseph Durlak, "Comparative Effectiveness of Paraprofessional and Professional Helpers," *Psychological Bulletin* 86, 1979, pp. 80-92.

10. Larry E. Beutler, Paulo P. P. Machado, and Susan Allstetter Neufeldt, "Therapist Variables" in *Handbook of Psychotherapy and Behavior Change, op. cit.*, p. 249.

11. Robyn Dawes, *House of Cards: Psychology and Psychotherapy Built on Myth*. New York: The Free Press/ Macmillan, Inc., 1994, pp. 101-102.

12. H. J. Eysenck, "Meta-Analysis Squared—Does It Make Sense?" *American Psychologist*, February 1995, p. 111.

13. "Ambiguity Pervades Research on Effectiveness of Psychotherapy," *Brain / Mind Bulletin*, October 4, 1982, p. 2.

14. Hans H. Strupp and Suzanne W. Hadley, "Specific vs. Nonspecific Factors in Psychotherapy," *Archives of General Psychiatry*, September 1979, p. 1126.

15. Hans Strupp, "The Tripartite Model and the *Consumer Reports* Study," *American Psychologist*, October 1996, p. 1021.

Chapter 4: The Rise & Practice of Problem-Centered Counseling

1. See Martin and Deidre Bobgan. *PsychoHeresy: The Psychological Seduction of Christianity* (1987); and Chapter 4 of *The End of "Christian Psychology"* (1997). Santa Barbara, CA: EastGate Publishers.

2. Robert C. Fuller. *Mesmerism and the American Cure of Souls*. Philadelphia: University of Pennsylvania Press, 1982, p. 104.

3. Freedheim, Donald K., ed. *History of Psychotherapy: A Century of Change*. Washington, DC: American Psychological Association, 1992, p. 32.

4. Thomas Szasz. *The Myth of Psychotherapy*. Garden City: Doubleday/Anchor Press, 1978, p. 43.

5. *Ibid.*, pp. 11-12.

6. Irwin Kutash and Alexander Wolf, eds. *Psychotherapist's Casebook: Theory and Technique in the Practice of Modern Therapies*. Northvale, NJ: Jason Aronson Inc., 1993. p. xiii.

7. *Ibid.*, p. xv.

8. See Martin and Deidre Bobgan. *Competent to Minister: The Biblical Care of Souls*. Santa Barbara, CA: EastGate Publishers, 1994, pp. 199-213; and *TheoPhostic Couneling: Divine Revelation or PsychoHeresy*, EastGate Publishers, 1999.

9. W. E. Vine. *The Expanded Vines: Expository Dictionary of New Testament Words*, John R. Kohlenberger III, ed. Minneapolis: Bethany House Publishers, 1984, p. 543.
10. *Ibid.*, p. 744.
11. Martin and Deidre Bobgan. *Against "Biblical Counseling": For the Bible*. Santa Barbara, CA: EastGate Publishers, 1994, pp. 73-87.
12. *Ibid.*
13. *PsychoHeresy Awareness Letter*, Vol. 5, No. 5, pp. 1-3.
14. Martin and Deidre Bobgan. *Four Temperaments, Astrology & Personality Testing*. Santa Barbara, CA: EastGate Publishers, 1992.
15. Bobgan, *Against "Biblical Counseling": For the Bible, op. cit.,* pp. 57ff.

Chapter 5: Christ-Centered Ministry or Problem-Centered Counseling?
1. Jay Lebow. "War of the Worlds: Researchers and practitioners collide on EMDR and CISD." *Psychotherapy Networker*, Vol. 27, No. 5., p. 79.

For a sample copy of a free newsletter about the intrusion of psychological counseling theories and therapies into the church, please write to:

**PsychoHeresy Awareness Ministries
4137 Primavera Road
Santa Barbara, CA 93110**

or call:

1-800-216-4696

<http://www.psychoheresy-aware.org>

Books by Martin & Deidre Bobgan

PSYCHOHERESY: The Psychological Seduction of Christianity exposes fallacies and failures of psychological counseling theories and therapies. Reveals anti-Christian biases, internal contradictions, and documented failures of secular psychotherapy; and examines amalgamations with Christianity and explodes firmly entrenched myths that undergird these unholy unions. 272 pages, softbound.

COMPETENT TO MINISTER: The Biblical Care of Souls calls Christians back to the Bible and mutual care in the Body of Christ, encourages personal ministry among Christians, and equips believers to minister God's grace through biblical conversation, prayer, and practical help. 252 pages, softbound.

THE END OF "CHRISTIAN PSYCHOLOGY" reveals that "Christian psychology" includes contradictory theories and techniques; describes and analyzes major psychological theories influencing Christians; shows that professional psychotherapy with its underlying psychologies is questionable at best, detrimental at worst, and a spiritual counterfeit at least; and challenges the church to rid itself of all signs and symptoms of this scourge. 290 pages, softbound.

AGAINST "BIBLICAL COUNSELING": FOR THE BIBLE reveals what biblical counseling is, rather than what it pretends or hopes to be. Its primary thrust is to call Christians back to the Bible and to biblically ordained ministries and mutual care in the Body of Christ. 200 pages, softbound.

HYPNOSIS: MEDICAL, SCIENTIFIC, OR OCCULTIC? examines hypnosis from scientific, historical, and biblical perspectives and shows that hypnosis is the same whether practiced by benevolent medical doctors, shamans, or occultists. The book exposes both obvious and hidden dangers. 144 pages, softbound.

FOUR TEMPERAMENTS, ASTROLOGY & PERSONALITY TESTING examines personality types and tests from a biblical, historical, and research basis and answers such questions as: Do the four temerpaments give true insight into people? Are personality inventories and tests valid ways of finding out about people? 214 pages, softbound.

More books by Martin & Deidre Bobgan

JAMES DOBSON'S GOSPEL OF SELF-ESTEEM & PSYCHOLOGY demonstrates that many of Dobson's teachings are based on godless, secular opinions. Self-esteem and psychology are the two major thrusts of his ministry that supercede sin, salvation, and sanctification. They are another gospel. 248 pages, softbound.

LARRY CRABB'S GOSPEL traces Crabb's 22-year journey of jolts, shifts, and expansions as he has sought to create the best combination of psychology and the Bible. Crabb's eclectic theories and methods remain psychologically bound and consistent with current psychotherapy trends. This book provides a detailed analysis. 210 pages, softbound.

12 STEPS TO DESTRUCTION: Codependency/Recovery Heresies examines codependency/recovery teachings, Alcoholics Anonymous, twelve-step groups, and addiction treatment programs from a biblical, historical, and research perspective and urges believers to trust in the sufficiency of Christ and the Word of God. 256 pages, softbound.

THEOPHOSTIC COUNSELING ~ Divine Revelation? or PsychoHeresy? examines a recovered memory therapy comprised of many existent psychological therapies and techniques, demon deliverance teachings, and elements from the inner healing movement, which include guided imagery, visualization, and hypnosis. 144 pages, softbound.

MISSIONS & PSYCHOHERESY exposes the mental health profession's false façade of expertise for screening missionary candidates and caring for missionaries. It explodes myths about psychological testing and reveals the prolific practice of using mental health professionals to provide care for missionaries suffering from problems of living. 168 pages, softbound.

CRI GUILTY OF PSYCHOHERESY? answers the CRI-Passantino "Psychology & the Church" series, exposes their illogical reasoning, and argues that supporting psychotherapy and its underlying psychologies is an opprobrium in the church. 152 pages, softbound.